# We Can Trust The Bible

## Helping Children Understand Where the Bible Came From

# Tim Lale

Pacific Press® Publishing Association

Nampa, Idaho
Oshawa, Ontario, Canada
www.pacificpress.com

Cover design by Gerald and Sharon Monks; adapted by Steve Lanto
Cover design resources from dreamstime.com / iStockphoto.com
Cover picture of Jesus by Darrel Tank
Edited and designed by Aileen Andres Sox
Inside art resources from iStockphoto, The Israel Museum, Jerusalem, Pacific Press®, and Wikimedia Commons

The author assumes full responsibility for the accuracy of all facts and quotations as cited in this book.

Library of Congress Cataloging-in-Publication Data:

Lale, Tim, 1964-
We can trust the Bible : helping children understand where the Bible came from / Tim Lale.
p. cm.
ISBN 13: 978-0-8163-2500-9 (pbk.)
ISBN 10: 0-8163-2500-6 (pbk.)
1. Bible—Juvenile literature.  I. Title.
BS539.L254 2011
220.6'1—dc23                                    2011048014

Additional copies of this book are available by
calling toll-free 1-800-765-6955 or by visiting http://www.adventistbookcenter.com.

12 13 14 15 16 • 5 4 3 2 1

# Table of Contents

1  We Can Trust the Bible .......... 7

2  The Two Big Parts of the Bible .......... 9

3  The Books of the Old Testament .......... 11

4  The Books of the New Testament .......... 14

5  How God Gave Us the Bible .......... 16

6  Storytellers Preserved the Bible .......... 19

7  The Alphabet Arrives on Time .......... 21

8  Moses Writes the Pentateuch .......... 24

9  Prophets and Scribes .......... 26

10  The Hebrew Bible and the Septuagint .......... 29

11  New Testament Writers .......... 32

12  Putting the Bible Together .......... 35

13  Jerome the Scribe .......... 38

14  The "Almost" Bible Writers .......... 41

15  The Bible in the Middle Ages .......... 43

16  The Waldensians .......... 47

17  The First English Bibles .......... 52

18  Gutenberg, Printing, and Bookmaking .......... 55

19  Mr. Erasmus, the Student of Greek .......... 58

20  Tyndale and the First English Bibles .......... 61

21  The King James Version of the Bible .......... 64

22  The Bible Comes to America .......... 67

23  Digging Up the Bible .......... 70

24  The Dead Sea Scrolls .......... 73

25  The Bibles of Today .......... 77

# Dedication

To my parents, Don and Ann Lale, for teaching me the Bible throughout my childhood and instilling in me the certainty that the Word of God is sacred and trustworthy. See you on the Day of the Lord.

# We Can Trust the Bible

You probably have a Bible. Did your mom or dad or grandmother give it to you? Your Bible may have a soft cover or a hard cover. It may have many pictures or no pictures. I have about ten Bibles at my house. My favorite one has a black leather cover and very thin, crinkly pages. Does your Bible have maps in the back?

The Bible is a special book. People talk about it being a message from God. They handle the Bible with care. Some people don't even like to put things on top of a Bible. Why is this Book so special?

The Bible is special because God gave it to us. He speaks to us through the words in it. Just as sure as God is sitting on His throne, the Bible is God's written message to us, His children.

You may be wondering, How did God give this book to us? He did not write it Himself. He did not hand it over to one person, already completed.

The story of how we got the Bible is long! It begins more than three thousand years ago. Can you imagine three thousand years? That's more years than I can even think about. But it is not a long time for God.

About forty people wrote the parts of the Bible. They lived at different times and in different places. That was not a problem for God. He knows every person who has ever lived. He knows how many hairs you have on your head! So it was easy for God to keep track of the Bible writers.

> **A Verse to Remember:**
> "*Every word of God is true. . . . Do not add to his words*" (Proverbs 30:5, 6, NCV).

You've heard or read the Bible stories, I'm sure. You know that Adam and Eve committed the first sin in the Garden of Eden. Later, some people tried to build the Tower of Babel to reach heaven. Noah built an ark and sailed it through the Flood, remember? And David killed a giant warrior named Goliath with a small stone and a slingshot. What exciting stories!

Christians say that they believe the stories in the Bible. They believe that Adam and Noah and David were real people. Why do they believe those stories? Can you trust what the Bible says? Should you listen to what it says? Should you obey what it commands?

God Himself tells us to believe and obey the words of the Bible. He says, Trust Me and you will live happily forever.

God had a purpose for giving us the Bible. He wanted us to know Him. The Bible stories tell us what God is like. We cannot see God until Jesus comes back to take us to heaven. The Bible helps us to see God without actually seeing Him.

Here is another purpose God had for the Bible. He wished to tell us how we can be saved from sin. Our Father in heaven wants us to live close to Him forever. We can do that only when we believe that Jesus died for us. Then our sins can be forgiven so our minds can be clean and ready for us to be with God.

From the Bible we can know that God is good and perfect. From the Bible we can know that He loves us very, very much. And from the Bible we can know God's plan to save us from our sins.

The Bible was written a long time ago. We can still trust it because God has protected it. He made sure that the Bible stayed the same over the years. It is still the same Book today.

## Teaching Tips

- If your child doesn't own a Bible, consider buying the *International Children's Bible,* used in Seventh-day Adventist elementary schools in North America, or a *New International Readers' Version.*
- Explore these Bible topics with your child: God's words give life—Deuteronomy 8:2–4; God's words are perfect—2 Samuel 22:31.
- Gather together all the Bibles in your home. Tell any stories about particular ones that come to mind. Share why you like and use a particular one.
- Begin helping your child to memorize the books of the Bible in order so that he or she becomes familiar with using it. (See page 80 for a handy list.) Song versions aid learning. One you may remember from your childhood is "The Books of the Bible" by Alfred P. Gibbs. An audio file is available at www.wholesomewords.org.

# The Two Big Parts of the Bible

Most Bibles are big, fat books. Your Bible may be the biggest book you own. Even if you can read very fast, you might not be able to read the whole thing in one year. Many Bibles have tiny writing and more than a thousand pages. That will keep you busy for a while.

You can trust the Bible. But to trust God's Book, you must know what is in it. The Bible is split into two parts, called the *Old Testament* and the *New Testament. Testament* is a long word that means covenant.

A *covenant* is an agreement between two people. In the Bible, the two agreements are between God and His people. The Old Testament is the old agreement. The New Testament is the new agreement.

You may wonder, Who are God's people? They are the ones who believe in God and accept His help.

What does it mean that God has an agreement with His people? Let's say your mother asks you to clean the cat litter box or the dog dish before you play outside. You say to her, "Yes, I'll do it." Now you have an agreement between you and your mom. You will clean up before you go to play.

In a similar way, God has an agreement with His people. He says, "If you will accept My help, I will save you from sin and death." And when God's people say, "Yes, we will accept Your help," then they have an agreement with God.

The books of the Old Testament tell about the first agreement God had with His people, after Adam and Eve sinned. The Old Testament books were written before Jesus was born.

The books of the New Testament were

> **A Verse to Remember:**
> *"All Scripture is given by God"*
> *(2 Timothy 3:16, ICB).*

written after Jesus was born. They tell us about the agreement between God and His people after Jesus died on the cross.

The first agreement God had was with the nation of Israel. The people agreed that God would take care of them. In turn, they would love and obey Him. Sadly, many people of Israel did not keep to the agreement. They wanted God's care but did not love and obey Him.

When Jesus came to live on earth, rebellious people hated Him. Can you imagine anyone hating the Son of God? Well, those people did. They had forgotten the old agreement.

After Jesus died on the cross, God made a new agreement. He said to people on earth, "If any of you will accept My Son Jesus to save you from sin, I will take care of you." Does that sound similar to the first agreement? It is very similar. Only this time, the agreement was between God and all people on earth.

The two sections of the Bible seem different from each other. But they are parts of the same story. The Old Testament is part one of God's plan to save people. The New Testament is part two of the plan.

We come to trust the Bible when we know what is in it.

*Jesus the Sacrifice*

Do you remember hearing that people in the Old Testament had to sacrifice animals? It seems like a gross thing to do. But offering a sacrifice was very important. The people of the Old Testament were sinful. They lived before Jesus came to earth. God told them to sacrifice an animal for their sin. The books of the Old Testament tell about that.

After Jesus died, God's people did not have to sacrifice animals anymore. Jesus had given Himself as the Sacrifice. After that, no more animal sacrifice was needed. The New Testament books talk about that.

## Teaching Tips

- Explore these Bible topics with your child: The faithful people of God wrote about Him—Malachi 3:16; Matthew connected the Old and New Testaments—Matthew 1:22, 23; where the promise of the Messiah, which God made in Eden when He spoke to the serpent (Genesis 3:15), is repeated by Jesus—John 3:16.
- Talk to your child about the history of the plan of salvation: God and Jesus agreed on the rescue plan long before sin came; They made the promise as soon as Adam and Eve sinned (Genesis 3:15); the old and new agreements between God and the Israelites were all part of the same plan.

# The Books of the Old Testament

Have you ever counted on your fingers? Maybe your toes as well? Sometimes I still do. One, two, three, four, five. My fingers make a handy counter.

If I want to count all the books in the Bible, I must count to sixty-six. That's the fingers and toes of three and a half people! The Old Testament contains thirty-nine of those sixty-six books. The books were written in Hebrew, the language of ancient Israel.

Jesus read and studied the Old Testament when He was a boy. In His time, the books were called the *Scriptures* or "the Law and the Prophets and the Writings." When Jesus asked people, "Have you never read in the Scriptures?" (Matthew 21:42, NKJV), He was talking about the Old Testament books.

The Old Testament begins with five books that are called the *Pentateuch* or books of the law. Moses either wrote or gathered the material in these five books.

• **Genesis** • **Exodus** • **Leviticus**
• **Numbers** • **Deuteronomy**

These five books tell us how the world began and how sin got started. They tell us what led up to the Flood of Noah's time. They tell about Abraham, the man God chose to start a new nation. In these books, we find out how God's new nation escaped from Pharaoh in Egypt and we can read the laws and instructions God gave to His people.

The next books of the Bible, twelve in all, we call *history books*. History is the story of what happened to a group of people and their leaders and kings. Books like

> **A Verse to Remember:** *"God promised this Good News long ago . . . , as it is written in the Holy Scriptures"* (Romans 1:2, NCV).

# Lift Up Your Biblia

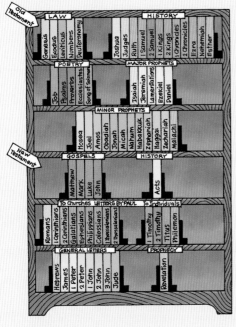

The Bible looks like one big book, but it is more than that. The name *Bible* comes from a Greek word, *biblia,* which means "books." This is a good name for God's Book. Why? Because the Bible is really a collection of sixty-six books. Some of the Bible's books, like the book of Isaiah, are long. Some, like the book of Titus, are very short. The books had forty different authors. When you pick up your Bible, you are picking up a whole bookcase!

Judges, 1 and 2 Samuel, and Nehemiah tell stories you probably know. Think of Joshua, Samson, King David, and Ruth. Think about the lives of King Saul and Solomon, Joash and Hezekiah. Their stories are in the history books:

**• Joshua • Judges • Ruth • 1 and 2 Samuel**
**• 1 and 2 Kings • 1 and 2 Chronicles**
**• Ezra • Nehemiah • Esther**

The story of Job comes in the middle of the Old Testament. Remember the man who lost everything and got sick besides? God made him well again. Job probably lived long before Abraham and the nation of Israel. No one knows who wrote down his story. The book of Job is tucked in with the books of poetry or what are sometimes called the *wisdom books.*

**• Job • Psalms • Proverbs**
**• Ecclesiastes • Song of Solomon**

King David and King Solomon wrote wise sayings, poems, and songs. To be wise means to know the truth. Being wise also means knowing God and what He is about. David and Solomon were wise and knew God very well. That is why their books ended up in the Bible.

The fourth part of the Old Testament we call the *Prophets.* The seventeen books written by prophets are filled with messages from God. The people of Israel needed reminding that they should be faithful and obedient to God. Somehow, they kept forgetting!

We call some of the prophets "major prophets" because they wrote more, not because what they wrote was more important. Isaiah and Jeremiah wrote the longest books of prophecies. For many years, they pleaded with the people of Israel to obey God. Sadly, the people rebelled instead. Most of them were captured by an army and taken to Babylon in chains.

You remember Daniel, the man who met the lions in their den? He was one of the greatest prophets ever. God gave him important messages about history and the coming of Jesus.

Later, Zechariah received a message from God in a vision, which is like a dream. God promised that He would bring His people back home. He also promised that they would rebuild the city of Jerusalem. And that is exactly what happened.

The prophets were important messengers. They faithfully delivered God's messages to His people. The messages said to God's people, if you will obey God, He can do the good things He has promised. The messages also said, if you rebel against God or ignore Him, you have shut Him out and He cannot do those good things. Sometimes the people listened, and sometimes they ignored God's words or rebelled against Him. We can learn from the Bible what happens when people obey God and what happens when they disobey. I want to be someone who listens to God and trusts Him, don't you?

## Teaching Tips

• Explore these Bible topics with your child: God's people obey His commandments—Deuteronomy 11:26–28; only God could make the Scriptures happen—Matthew 19:26; the best use of the Bible—Colossians 3:16.

• Sometimes children gloss over the key words in what is read to them, because they don't yet know the meaning. Explain to your child the following words: *history, language, testament, prophet.*

• Play the game Egypt to Canaan (available from www.adventistbookcenter.com). As you play, talk about the plan God had for the Israelites. Especially emphasize how it was part of the bigger plan to save the people of the world from sin.

• Ask your child which Bible stories they remember. Find and show them the references in the Bible. This can become a game of "Can Mom or Dad find the story?"

# The Books of the New Testament

Have you ever gotten up early to watch the sun rise? I love to see the sun come up for a new day. The golden colors of the world get brighter and brighter every minute. When the sun comes up, I have to feel good!

In a similar way, a sunrise happened for God's people when Jesus was born in Bethlehem. After many dark years of not having the Messiah come to them, finally the bright day came. The second half of the Bible, called the New Testament, tells about the sunrise for God's people.

One way we know the Bible can be trusted is this: the Old Testament announced Jesus' coming many times. Hundreds of years before Jesus was born, the prophets wrote messages about it. The prophet Micah wrote, "Bethlehem, you might not be an important town in the nation of Judah. But out of you will come a ruler over Israel for me" (Micah 5:2, NIrV).

Micah's message from God came true when Jesus was born in Bethlehem. When did Micah receive this promise from God? About four hundred years before the birth of Jesus!

The first four books of the New Testament tell the story of Jesus' life. They are Matthew, Mark, Luke, and John. We call them the *Gospels*. But why four books to tell the same story?

Mark was one of the first Christian believers. He wrote the story down quite soon after Jesus went back to heaven. Matthew and John were disciples with Jesus. They

> **A Verse to Remember:**
> *"I will make you and the woman enemies to each other. . . . Her child will crush your head"* (Genesis 3:15, ICB).

wrote their books later, using Mark's book to help them. Luke was a doctor. He was also a careful researcher. He gathered the true stories of Jesus' life from people who knew Him well. Luke also got help from Mark's book. The parts of the four books that are the same help us to see something important. They show us that all four books tell the true story of Jesus.

The disciples got busy after Jesus went back to heaven. The book of Acts is filled with their stories. The disciples preached the good news about Jesus in many places. They baptized thousands of new believers. Some of the disciples, like Peter and Paul, traveled to distant places and even put up with going to prison. They wanted everyone possible to be invited to accept Jesus. This exciting book called Acts was written by Luke.

The New Testament contains twenty-one letters. You are not reading someone's personal mail, however. Paul, Peter, and John wrote letters to the churches they had started. The church members needed to be encouraged to stay true to Jesus. They needed help to understand God's ways. The letters were passed around. Copies of the letters were sent from one church to another. It's not surprising that these wonderful letters became part of the Bible.

The last book in the New Testament, called *Revelation,* is also the last book of the Bible. Revelation tells us what will happen to our world in the future. The disciple John wrote down what he saw in visions God showed him. The messages in Revelation help us know how God will get rid of sin forever. Perhaps most important, John explained how Jesus would soon come to take us home with Him.

The Bible begins with the book of Genesis. In that book, we read the promise that Jesus would come to earth the first time and save us from sin. The Bible ends with the book of Revelation. In there we read the promise that Jesus will come a second time to take us to heaven. We can trust the Bible because it is filled with God's promises from beginning to end. God keeps His promises!

## Teaching Tips

- Explore these Bible topics with your child: A careful writer gathered the Gospel of Luke—Luke 1:3, 4; truth comes through spoken and written words—2 Thessalonians 2:15; we are blessed by doing what God's Book says—Revelation 22:7.
- Play the game Life of Paul (available from www.adventistbookcenter.com).

# How God Gave Us the Bible

My favorite joke when I was a boy goes like this:

Q: How many elephants can you fit into a Mini Cooper?

A: Four: two in the front, two in the back.

Q: How many giraffes can you fit into a Mini Cooper?

A: None. It's full of elephants.

My dad told me that joke about forty years ago, when I was six. Sometimes I tell the joke with slightly different words. But the joke is always pretty much the same.

The Bible books were written much longer ago than forty years. They were written over a period of more than one thousand six hundred years. But that was not a problem for God. He gave the messages to each author, and the authors wrote them down in their own words. But the main idea is always pretty much the same.

Moses wrote his five books more than one thousand two hundred years *before* Jesus was born. The

King David was a Bible writer. He wrote many poems that were used in worship. They can be found in the book of Psalms.

disciple John wrote his books about ninety years *after* Jesus was born. Did Moses and John write different words? Yes. But did they write similar messages? Yes! From beginning to end, the Bible's authors wrote about God's plan of salvation.

Do you trust the Bible? You can if you know how God gave it to us. The Bible itself tells us how this happened. The apostle Paul said, "God has breathed life into all of Scripture" (2 Timothy 3:16, NIrV).

God decided not to give the writers the exact words to write down. He wanted people to tell the stories about His love in their own words.

The Bible writers got busy when the Holy Spirit of God prompted them. The disciple Peter said, "No prophecy in the Scriptures ever comes from the prophet's own interpretation. No prophecy ever came from what a man wanted to say, but men led by the Holy Spirit spoke words from God" (2 Peter 1:20, 21, ICB). Why did Peter call the writing *prophecy*? Because prophecy means messages from God.

The writers received messages in many different ways. Moses met God on Mount Sinai. God gave him a piece of stone with the Ten Commandments written on it. But most of the Bible writers did not receive a message right from God's hand!

Some writers like Daniel had a dream. Others like Samuel heard the voice of God speaking. Once in a while, a writer like Ezekiel had a vision from God, which is like having a dream while you are awake. The usual way a writer received a message from God was through his or her thoughts.

You remember that many of the Old Testament books are history books. The writers of history books, such as Joshua, Samuel, and Ezra, used records written down by others to help them write. Families kept written records of their great, great-great, and great-great-great-grandparents. Kings kept records of the battles and other events of their reigns. The Bible writers looked at those records so that they had their facts straight. God wanted the books to be right and true.

> **A Verse to Remember:**
> *"In the past God spoke to our ancestors through the prophets. He spoke to them many times and in many different ways"* (Hebrews 1:1, ICB).

To whom did God give His messages? The people of Israel, also known as the Jews. Paul said, "The Jews have been given the very words of God" (Romans 3:2, NIrV). We can trust that God sent the messages to the Bible writers. And we can trust the Bible because we know how God gave it to us.

*A long time coming*

The Bible writers did not know that their book would be included in the Bible. Each person wrote the messages given by God for the time they lived in. The putting together of the books to make the whole Bible came much later, after all the writers had died. Can you imagine how surprised Joshua or David would be to see a big Bible? We can trust the Bible because all the writers wrote down their messages faithfully as God gave them.

David wrote many beautiful songs called Psalms. Not all the psalms in the book of Psalms are David's, however. If the author is known, it is listed at the top of each psalm. Here's part of a psalm that David did write:

"Forgive me for my secret sins.
Keep me from the sins I want to do.
Don't let them rule me.
Then I can be pure and free
    from the greatest of sins.
I hope my words and thoughts please you.
Lord, you are my Rock,
    the one who saves me"
        (Psalm 19:12–14, ICB).

## Teaching Tips

• Explore these Bible topics with your child: Sometimes God spoke out loud—Exodus 19:19; many times God spoke through dreams—Genesis 28:11–13; God used a chest plate with different colored stones to show the priests what He wanted Israel to do—Numbers 27:21.

• Discuss with your child some of the many different ways God has spoken to people. Affirm his or her sense of God's direct contact with us. Among the ways to talk about are dreams and visions, thoughts given by the Holy Spirit, God's audible voice, messages from angels, and the words of Jesus while He was on earth.

• Have your child draw Mount Sinai and Moses receiving the Ten Commandments directly from God Himself.

# Storytellers Preserved the Bible

My grandfather, Sidney Alfred Lale, was born in 1900. When the Great War began in 1914, he was only fourteen years old. The war continued until 1918. Grandpa Lale was too young to be a soldier in the Great War. However, when he was seventeen, he was allowed to join the Home Guard.

He was one of many teenagers who wore a uniform and stood guard at night near their homes. Grandpa was also allowed to carry a gun.

My father told me one story from Grandpa's duty as a wartime guard. One night, Grandpa heard sounds like footsteps. He shouted, "Halt! Who goes there?" But the footsteps kept coming.

In Bible times, a good storyteller could learn thirty thousand lines of poetry, the size of a big book today. Many of the people listening also knew all those lines. If the storyteller added something extra or left something out, someone would say, "No, that's not right!" And the storyteller would have to go back and tell the story correctly. For hundreds of years after Moses wrote the first five Bible books, the Israelites still loved to listen to storytellers. This picture shows Bedouins camped at an oasis more than two hundred years ago. Perhaps they are telling stories like the Israelites did.

Grandpa fired his gun into the air. Then he heard the sound of footsteps running away. In the morning, he found out that it was a donkey!

The stories of the Bible come to us both by speaking and by writing. Through the years and centuries of Adam and Noah, the people knew about God and His ways. They knew the stories of God creating the world, Adam's and Eve's sin, the Flood, and the Tower of Babel. No one had invented a pencil or paper. No one knew how to write! And yet, the stories were never lost.

How did parents pass on the knowledge of God to their children and grandchildren? The facts and events were told as stories, poems, and songs. The stories and poems were also performed by storytellers. A storyteller learned thousands of lines of poetry. At a special time, a storyteller stood in front of a big crowd of people and recited the stories everyone remembered.

Did the stories change as they were told and retold? No. Storytellers had learned the words as though they were a song. Every word had to be correct! No changes were allowed. Each time the story was told, it sounded the same. The people loved to hear those old stories.

For hundreds of years, until the time of Moses, families told the stories about God and His wonderful deeds. They never forgot any of the parts of the stories. When God asked Moses to write all the stories down, lots of people could help him get them right.

We can trust the Bible because God helped His people to remember the stories of the beginning of the world. He helped them to remember exactly what had happened, and nothing important was lost.

## Teaching Tips

• Explore these Bible topics with your child: Someone kept records that helped the Bible writers—1 Chronicles 4:22; people remembered important stories and passed them on—Genesis 10:1; God's good deeds cannot stay hidden—Isaiah 63:7

• Find a small notebook to keep a diary with your child. At the end of each day, ask him or her to tell you what happened to him or her that he or she remembers. Explain that you are helping him or her collect stories about his or her life.

• Prepare a Bible story to tell your child by reading it carefully and memorizing the main details. After telling the story, remind your child that most Israelites knew about God because they heard someone tell the true stories about Him and His people in ancient times.

• For morning worships in your home, begin a series of "Let's figure out what good thing God has done." Find a new one every day.

# The Alphabet Arrives on Time

Did you ever sing the alphabet song with the tune that sounds like "Twinkle, twinkle, little star"? My three daughters sang the alphabet song hundreds of times in the car. "Now I know my ABCs. Next time won't you sing with me?" I will never forget that song!

Cuneiform

Long, long ago, people did not know how to write words. Then, before even Abraham was born, someone in the ancient city of Sumer used a sharp stone to make little pictures in wet clay. This was the first kind of writing, called *cuneiform*, which means picture writing.

The ancient Egyptian people used picture writing. Sometimes they scratched or carved pictures into a stone. Look at the Egyptian writing below. Do you see an eye? What else can you see?

The picture writing of the Egyptians is not an alphabet. It does not use letters put together as words. So where did alphabet writing come from?

In 1905, an Englishman named Sir Flinders Petrie found some writing near Mount Sinai.

Egyptian picture writing

The writing he found was written long ago by Canaanites. Before Moses was born, the Canaanites worked in mines on the mountain. They invented the first alphabet that was used to write whole words. As time went by, the alphabet spread to other countries nearby. It was called the *Semitic alphabet.*

God was preparing the way for Moses to write the first five books of the Bible. You remember that Moses grew up in the court of Pharaoh in Egypt. He must have learned how to write with Egyptian picture writing. But he also learned the Semitic alphabet. When God told Moses to write down the laws and history for the people of Israel, Moses was ready to do just that.

You might imagine Moses writing on paper. But paper was not invented until long after that. Moses used papyrus instead.

*Papyrus* is a little like thick paper. It was made from the stem of a sedge plant that grew by the Nile River. The plant stems were smashed flat, dried, and glued together to make long rolls. The long roll of papyrus was called a *scroll.*

Papyrus sheets are very strong and and can last a long time. You can see many papyrus scrolls in museums today. Some of them are more than three thousand years old!

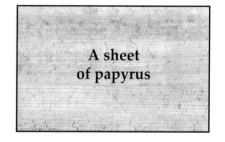

**A sheet of papyrus**

How did Moses write those long books? He wrote with a stylus. A *stylus* was a sharp stick or a pointed piece of bone. Moses dipped the stylus in ink and wrote on the papyrus.

Where did he get the ink from? The Egyptians made black ink from plants stems, soot, and water. First, they dried and crushed plant stems into a powder. Then they mixed the powder with black soot in a little bit of water. The black liquid sat in a small, rectangular wooden container.

The Egyptians also made red ink. Instead of using black soot for color, they mixed dirt called *red ocher* into the ink. Moses wrote with the ink that Egyptians knew how to make.

We can trust the Bible because God placed the tools and materials for it to be written. He put them in the right part of the world at just the right time.

### The mighty papyrus plant

The basket that Moses' mother, Jochebed, made for him when he was a baby was woven from papyrus plants. The plants grew by the Nile River. They were ten to sixteen feet (three to six meters) tall. The stem was a triangle shape. This shape is very strong!

Moses' mother cut the stems into short strips and wove them together. The papyrus plant kept Moses safe when he was a baby. Years later, the plant gave Moses a kind of paper to write on when he was old.

### How do we know Moses wrote Genesis?

You might wonder, Did Moses really write the book of Genesis? How could he write about all the events that happened before he was born? We know Moses wrote Genesis for two reasons. One is that storytellers had kept the old stories from being changed or forgotten. The second

reason is that Jesus Himself called the Pentateuch "the book of Moses." Jesus said, "Haven't you read in the scroll of Moses the story of the [burning] bush?" (Mark 12:26, NIrV). We know that Genesis and Exodus were written by the same person. If Moses wrote Exodus where we read the burning bush story as Jesus said he did, he also wrote Genesis.

## Teaching Tips

• Explore these Bible topics with your child: Papyrus reeds grew where there was lots of water—Job 8:11; boats were made out of papyrus—Isaiah 18:2; some of the ancient Israelites knew how to write—Joshua 18:4.

• Help your child to invent some picture characters to tell a story. For instance, to retell the story of Daniel in the lions' den, you can draw lions, simple praying hands, a crown (for the king), and a couple of simple faces for the evil conspirators. You can tell the story out loud, holding up the pictures, or create a poster that tells the story. You have created your own cuneiform!

• Find pictures of writing utensils from the past, such as the stylus, the quill, and the ink pen. Talk about how God has made sure that His prophets have always had the tools they need to write down His words.

• Try making small boats out of natural material. Some materials to try are bark, reeds, Popsicle sticks, or large leaves. Test their floating capabilities at a pond. Be sure to discuss the small basket that Moses was laid in, and how well it floated until Moses was rescued.

# Moses Writes the Pentateuch

We can trust the Bible because God made it happen. The first part of the Bible was written by Moses. He was the first leader of the nation of Israel. God told Moses to write down the laws and history.

Moses grew up in the court of Pharaoh, the king of Egypt. He received a good education and knew how to write. God was preparing him to be the leader of His people.

Moses lived sometime in the fifteenth century B.C. That means more than one thousand four hundred years before Jesus was born. That's a long, long time before Jesus!

The people of Israel were slaves in Egypt when Moses was born. God had a plan to rescue the whole nation from slavery. He chose Moses to lead the people away from Egypt and back to Canaan. God had promised Canaan as their home long before.

As soon as the people of Israel were safely away from Egypt, God told Moses to "record their journey" (Numbers 33:2, NIrV). Moses must have written a diary. Faithfully, he wrote down the adventures of the Israelites in the desert for forty years.

Moses wrote by hand with a stylus and ink on papyrus or a leather scroll. A leather scroll was made from stretched leather. It was cut into strips and sewn together to make one long scroll.

> **A Verse to Remember:**
> *"Take this Scroll of the Law. Place it beside the ark of the covenant of the* LORD *your God"* (Deuteronomy 31:26, NIrV).

No papyrus or leather scroll written by Moses still exists today. We only have later copies.

Exodus 17 is the first time in the Bible God tells someone to write. God helped Joshua, Moses' assistant, and some Israelite soldiers to fight against an army from the city of Amalek. While Moses held up his hands in the air, Joshua's men defeated the Amalekites. The Israelites had won a great battle. "Then the Lord said to Moses, 'Write about this battle in a book so people will remember' " (Exodus 17:14, ICB).

Besides a diary, Moses wrote down long lists of laws. God wanted the people of Israel to offer sacrifices according to strict rules. He also wanted the people to be healthy. The laws commanded such things as "wash yourself regularly" and "keep sick people away from healthy people." God knew that sometimes people would hurt each other or steal things. The laws God gave would help the people to know what is right and wrong.

How did Moses find out about these laws? God gave all of them to him while he was on top of Mount Sinai. Moses wrote them down so that the laws would never be forgotten.

It's always a good idea to store something valuable in a place where you will never forget it. That's what Moses told the Levites to do. The Levites were the men who looked after the tabernacle all through the forty years in the desert. Moses instructed them, "Take this Scroll of the Law. Place it beside the ark of the covenant of the LORD your God" (Deuteronomy 31:26, NIrV). Because the scroll was sitting beside the ark of the covenant in the tabernacle, it would not get forgotten or lost.

What Moses wrote is called the *Pentateuch,* which is the first five books of the Bible. The Pentateuch is really one book divided into five parts. After the book was finished and put together, the people of Israel called it the book of the Law.

We can trust even the oldest parts of the Bible. God made clear how it should be written and how it should be kept safe.

## Teaching Tips

- Explore these Bible topics with your child: God's laws given to Moses—Exodus 24:3; God's agreement with Israel—Leviticus 26:46; Joseph and Mary and the Law of Moses—Luke 2:22; Jesus and the burning bush—Luke 20:37.
- Take some time to talk with your child about the benefits of good hygiene habits. Link them to the laws God gave to Moses for the people of Israel so that they would not become sick.
- Read the story from Exodus 17 of the battle the Israelites won because of Moses' arms being held up. Explain why the victory was God's. (Moses holding up his arms was a sign he allowed God to be in charge.)

# Prophets and Scribes

When I was your age, my favorite party game was Telephone. My dad would whisper something in my ear. He might say, "The corn will grow tall this year." Then I whispered it to my friend Sandy. Sandy whispered what he heard to Sarah. And Sarah whispered it to Derek. Derek whispered it to Colin. Finally, the message came to my brother Andrew. Andrew said, "I know what the message is! 'Dirt ball go brink man ear.' " Then we fell on the floor laughing.

The message in the books of the Bible has never been lost like we lost the message when we played Telephone. Starting with the books of Moses, the book of the Law was kept by the golden ark in the tabernacle. The Ten Commandments stones that God gave to Moses were kept inside the ark.

Over the years, leaders and prophets wrote down what happened to the people of Israel. The new scrolls were added to the book of the Law. We can trust the Bible because God's people took special care of the sacred books.

We can also trust the Bible because God spoke in the same way to many prophets. Many of the prophets said words like this: "Here is what God says." When the people followed what God's prophets wrote down, they lived safe and happy lives. When they didn't follow those words from God, bad things happened to them and their whole country.

What if someone said they had a message from God but they were lying? God told Moses how to test the prophet's words. "Sometimes a prophet will announce something in the name of the LORD. And it won't take place or come true. Then that's a message the LORD hasn't told him to speak" (Deuteronomy 18:22, NIrV). The false

**A Verse to Remember:**
*The LORD said to Joshua, "Never stop reading this Scroll of the Law. . . . Do everything that is written in it"*
*(Joshua 1:8, NIrV).*

messages were not added to the sacred scrolls.

The books that told the history (stories) of Israel were added to the book of the Law. You remember how Joshua led the Israelites into Canaan. Joshua "recorded those things in the Scroll of the Law of God" (Joshua 24:26, NIrV). And the prophet Samuel "explained to the people what the king who ruled over them should do. He wrote it down on a scroll. He placed it in front of the LORD in the [tabernacle]" (1 Samuel 10:25, NIrV). The prophets Samuel, Nathan, and Gad wrote the history of King David. And so the history books of Israel became part of the book of the Law.

Later prophets read the books of the earlier prophets as their Bible. Daniel read Jeremiah's book. That's how he knew when the captivity of the Israelites in Babylon would end. "I learned from the Scriptures," Daniel wrote, "that Jerusalem would remain destroyed for 70 years" (Daniel 9:2, NIrV). For Daniel, the Bible was the books of Moses and the writings of the prophets before him.

In the year 586 B.C., which means five hundred and eighty-six years before Christ was born, King Nebuchadnezzar destroyed Jerusalem. The temple built by Solomon was knocked down. Most of the Israelite people were taken captive to Babylon. What happened to the Scriptures that had been kept safe in the temple? The Levites, the men who worked in the temple, saved the scrolls. They took them with them to Babylon.

Some Levites began to write copies of the Scriptures. They gave the copies to Israelites living in different parts of Babylon. That way the scattered Israelite people could read the Scripture scrolls and stay true to God.

A Levite who wrote out copies of the Scriptures was called a *scribe.* A scribe had to follow strict rules for copying the Scriptures. One special rule was that the scribe had to find the middle word in that big set of books. If the middle word was correct, the scribe could be sure that he had not added or left out words by mistake.

The scribes became famous for their careful work. We can trust the Bible because God inspired the scribes to follow strict rules for making copies of the Scripture scrolls.

*Baruch the faithful scribe*
Baruch was a scribe who wrote things down for the prophet Jeremiah. God had told Jeremiah

to record all of his messages. While Jeremiah spoke the words, Baruch wrote them on a scroll.

You might think Baruch's job was done after he wrote everything. But God had told Jeremiah, "The scroll must be read aloud to the people of Israel." Jeremiah was under house arrest and could not go to the temple. He sent Baruch to read to the people. Because Baruch was a faithful scribe who loved God, he obeyed.

The son of an official from the court of King Jehoiakim heard Baruch read the scroll in the temple. The son asked Baruch to read the scroll secretly to the king's other officials. When the officials heard the messages from God, which said that Jerusalem would be destroyed, they were afraid. King Jehoiakim had rebelled against God. The officials told Baruch that he and Jeremiah should hide from the king.

When King Jehoiakim heard about the scroll, he demanded that it be brought to him. One of

his officials began to read the scroll. King Jehoiakim cut off pieces of the scroll with a knife and threw them into a fire. He ordered the officials to arrest Jeremiah and Baruch. But Prophet Jeremiah and his scribe had gone into hiding. No one could find them.

God spoke to Jeremiah again. "Get another scroll. Write on it all of the words that were on the first one. King Jehoiakim burned that one up" (Jeremiah 36:28, NIrV). Baruch and Jeremiah started all over again. Together, they made a new scroll like the first one. God's messages in the scroll could not be destroyed.

## Teaching Tips

• Explore these Bible topics with your child: Jeremiah writes a book—Jeremiah 36:2; a seven-day feast for the Law—Nehemiah 8.

• Do a Google search to find pictures of the Israelite tabernacle and the ark of the covenant. If necessary, refamiliarize yourself with the sections of the tent, the vessels and their uses, and the procedure for sacrifices. Show your child what went on in the tabernacle.

• Having the pictures and explaining the sacrifices will give you an opportunity to explain the plan of salvation in which Jesus became the Sacrifice for us all. Read Hebrews 9:24 about the Sanctuary in heaven. Ask, What is the difference between a copy and the original?

# The Hebrew Bible and the Septuagint

The books of the Old Testament were written over hundreds of years, which is a long, long time. The Levites, the men who looked after God's temple, faithfully cared for the scrolls after each one was written. The books that they considered to be messages from God, the Levites kept. The books that did not seem to be from God were not included in the Scriptures.

We can trust the Old Testament. Why? Because the books written first have the same language as the books written last. All of the words in the scrolls were written in the Hebrew language, except for a couple of pages. The language did not change for a thousand years! The scribes thought that the words of the scrolls were holy and sacred. That means they thought the words were very, very important and came from God. None of

This Hebrew torah was copied about one thousand years after Jesus was born. Hebrew is read from right to left. How do we read English?

> **A Verse to Remember:**
> *"I will put my teachings in their minds. And I will write them on their hearts. I will be their God, and they will be my people"* (Jeremiah 31:33, ICB).

# A Bible in Silver

Photo © The Israel Museum, Jerusalem

The oldest piece of the Bible we have today is a part of the book of Numbers. It was written on very thin pieces of silver called *silver leaf*, six hundred years before Jesus was born, or around the year 600 B.C. An *archaeologist*, someone who digs holes to find old treasures, discovered the pieces of silver leaf near Jerusalem in 1979. The priest's blessing is written on the tiny scroll:

"May the LORD bless you
and take good care of you.
May the LORD smile on you
and be gracious to you.
May the LORD look on you with favor
and give you his peace"
(Numbers 6:24–26, NIrV).

the scribes would dare to change a word in the scrolls. So the Hebrew language stayed almost the same for hundreds of years.

After seventy years of captivity in Babylon, some of the Israelites returned to Jerusalem. Now they spoke a language called Aramaic. The people did not use the Hebrew language anymore. But the two languages are quite similar. Israelite people still understood the Hebrew words of the book of the Law. God made sure the people knew about Him and His love.

Many more of the Israelites stayed behind in Babylon. Later, King Darius defeated the Babylonian armies, and he renamed the country Persia. Two hundred years after that, Alexander the Great conquered Persia. He made it part of the Greek Empire. The Israelites now had a Greek ruler, and they learned the Greek language. How could they read the Hebrew books of the Law and the Prophets if they spoke Greek?

During that time, the Greeks had a ruler named Ptolemy II. The king loved wisdom and books. He built a huge library in the city of Alexandria. He wanted to include the Hebrew books of the Law and the Prophets in his library. He also wanted to read the books in Greek. Although we don't know for sure, it seems that

Ptolemy caused the first translation of the book of the Law. That means he found some Israelite scribes who could write down the Hebrew books in the Greek language.

The book that Ptolemy had in Greek was the Pentateuch, the five books of the law written by Moses. The book was called the *Septuagint*. The word *septuagint* means seventy. An ancient Greek document says that Ptolemy paid seventy scribes to write the Greek version of the book of the Law. That's how the book got its name of Septuagint.

In later years, the Hebrew books of history, the prophets, and King David's psalms were translated into Greek. Before Jesus was born, all of the Hebrew books were placed in the Septuagint. This was the Bible of the time of Jesus.

Here's a good reason we can trust the Bible: God protected the sacred books through the times of change in Israel's history. He watched over them from the time of Babylon, through the years of Persia, to the time of the Greeks. The books of messages from God stayed with the Jewish scribes. At just the right time, the books were ready for people to read in their own language.

# Teaching Tips

- Explore some of the old books that helped the Bible writers: Book of the Wars of the Lord—Numbers 21:14; Book of Jashar—Joshua 10:12, 13; Book of the Annals of the Kings of Israel—1 Kings 14:19; Book of the Annals of the Kings of Judah—1 Kings 14:29; Book of the Kings of Israel and Judah—2 Chronicles 27:7.

- Begin to talk to your child about what "holy" means. For a child's understanding, that probably means limiting the discussion to holy things being separate, pure, special, and treated with extra respect. Include the idea that God is all of those things, and He is the Most Holy One of all.

- Locate printed material or Web sites in several different languages, such as Spanish, French, and German, to show your child what the languages look like. Some children have not figured out that they speak English as opposed to another language. Then talk to your child about the languages of the Bible (Hebrew, Aramaic, Greek). Find examples of those languages online (Hebrew is on page 29 of this book), to show what they look like.

- Consider purchasing a Bible history book. Many such books for children are available. The pictures of Jerusalem, Babylon, Media-Persia, and other places will help your child to place the Bible stories as he or she hears them.

# New Testament Writers

When Jesus died on the cross, the disciples were very sad. A few days later, many of the disciples saw Jesus alive again. Now they were very happy! Did those men and women keep quiet about seeing Jesus again? Oh no. They told everyone they met.

The eleven disciples saw Jesus rise into the air and go back to heaven. What stayed behind with them? All the words and actions of Jesus that they remembered.

Jesus had not told the disciples to write down what He said. He did not write things down either. The disciples did not write the parables and miracles and sayings of Jesus for many years after He left.

You may wonder why Jesus' followers did not write down everything about Jesus after He left. Remember, Jesus had told the people He would come right back. The disciples thought He would come back in a few months or years. They saw no need to write anything down.

We can trust the Bible because some people who knew Jesus told His stories the same way every time. They became like the storytellers of ancient Hebrew times. The New Testament writer named Luke said, "Reports of these things [about Jesus] were handed down to us. There were people who saw these things for themselves from the beginning and then passed the word on" (Luke 1:1, 2, NIrV).

Hundreds and thousands of people had heard Jesus speak. They knew who Jesus had healed and how He healed them. They remembered Jesus' parables. The people listening to the storytellers knew when they were telling the truth about Jesus.

Do you remember how God guided the Old Testament prophets in their writing? God's Holy Spirit showed them what to say. The Holy Spirit helped the New Testament writers too. Jesus promised His disciples: "[The Holy Spirit] will teach you all things. He will remind you of everything I have said to you" (John 14:26, NIrV).

About twenty years after Jesus went back to heaven, the apostle Paul began to write long letters. When Paul began his ministry, he had preached the gospel to the people. Now he wanted to send reminders about Jesus to the churches he had started. He could not visit the churches often because they were far apart. He sent letters instead.

Other disciples wrote letters to the churches. We can read two letters by Peter and three by John. Jesus' brother James wrote a letter also.

During this time, some people began to collect the stories and sayings of Jesus and write them down. Four books tell the story of Jesus: Matthew, Mark, Luke, and John. The short book written by Mark came first, probably about twenty years after Jesus went back to heaven. Two of the other writers, Matthew and Luke, seem to have read the book of Mark before they wrote their own book.

Dr. Luke wrote Luke and Acts.

Matthew's book begins with a list of parents and children, called a *genealogy*. This list of parents and children starts with Abraham and goes all the way down to Jesus. It helps to show how the Gospel books follow from the Old Testament books.

Luke was a doctor as well as a writer. He wrote his book about Jesus for the non-Jewish people who might not understand the Jewish religion so well. Luke did lots of homework before he began to write. He wanted to tell the truth about Jesus.

The disciple named John wrote a book about Jesus. When he was very old, John heard and saw messages from

**This portion of Matthew is from the oldest complete copy of the New Testament we have today: the Codex Sinaiticus (from the word *Sinai*).**

CODEX SINAITICUS.
MATTH. 10, 17.

God about the end of the world. Even though the messages scared him, John wrote them down faithfully. Now we can read those messages, too, in John's book called *Revelation*.

The followers of Jesus became known as Christians. The Christians read the books and letters written by the disciples and apostles. They realized that the books and letters were messages from God, just like the messages of the prophets in the Old Testament.

By the year A.D. 367, church members had decided which books were from God. A church leader named Athanasius made an official list. The New Testament was complete.

## What's a codex?

The first New Testament books were written on long papyrus scrolls or leather scrolls.

More than a hundred years after Jesus went back to heaven, Christians tried something new. They wanted to make new copies of the books that could be carried to many cities to be read. They cut papyrus into sheets and wrote on both sides of the sheets.

When a Christian scribe had completed the copy of a whole book, the sheets were piled together and glued or tied with a piece of wood on the top and a piece of wood on the bottom. This *codex* looked a bit like a modern-day book. All of the copies of the New Testament that we still have today are in the form of a codex.

# Teaching Tips

- Explore these Bible topics with your child: The other works of Jesus—John 21:25; Paul's instructions for his letters—1 Thessalonians 5:27; a saying of Jesus not found in the Gospels—Acts 20:35.
- For a Sabbath activity, try making a codex with your child. You will need individual sheets of three-hole paper, two pieces of flat board, an electric drill, and some twine. Thin plywood makes a good codex cover. If your child can write, have him or her write out some favorite verses on all the sheets of paper. Place a piece of paper on each board and mark where the holes should go. Drill at each mark. Place the sheets between the boards, and thread short lengths of twine through the holes. Tie them, but not so tightly that the codex won't open.

# Putting the Bible Together

Have you ever written a book? My daughter Megan wrote a book in the fourth grade. In her story, a girl took an alligator home from school for the weekend. The alligator's name was Gargle, and he wore a red collar. Megan drew pictures of the schoolgirl and Gargle the alligator. Megan's teacher helped her put the pages together inside a cover. In the end, my daughter had made a book of her own.

You may ask, How were all the Bible books put together? How did we get the Bible we have now, all inside one cover? After all, the writers of the Bible books lived in different times and different places. Many of them never met each other.

Something strange happened to the Old Testament books. They ended up in two completely different Bibles! The Jewish religion placed the Old Testament books in one cover. Nothing more was added. The Jewish elders met at a place called Jamnia in the year A.D. 90, which means ninety years after Christ was born. They agreed that for Jews, the thirty-nine Old Testament books were the whole Bible. When the books were gathered together into one big book, they became known as the Hebrew Bible.

For Christians, who believed in Jesus as their Savior from sin, the Old Testament books were only part one of the Bible. About two hundred years after Jesus was on earth, the New Testament books were collected to make part two of the Bible. Christians believe that the Bible is part one and part two together. We can trust the Bible because God directed how the Old Testament and the New Testament should be put together.

> **A Verse to Remember:**
> *"I have hidden your word in my heart so that I won't sin against you"* (Psalm 119:11, NIrV).

**Even from prison the apostle Paul wrote letters to the churches he started. His letters were copied many times and saved. They are in our Bibles today.**

The books of the New Testament were chosen in a unusual way. The disciples and other leaders of the church were called *apostles*. In the years after Jesus went back to heaven, some people wrote things that they claimed were written by the apostles. But Christians knew which letters and books were written by the apostles and which ones were not.

In the second century, or two hundred years, after Jesus went to heaven, the Christians made a list of books that they knew were written by apostles. Those books would be the New Testament. All the other books and letters were not allowed into the New Testament.

The early Christians wrote the first complete Bibles on papyrus scrolls, in a similar way to the ancient Old Testament books. All of the copies were in the Greek language. After about the year A.D. 150, the complete Bible was copied on papyrus sheets and made into a codex. Do you

remember the codex we talked about in the last chapter? A codex was a pile of papyrus sheets joined together between two pieces of wood. It looked like a book you could make at home.

Then in later years, the Bible was copied onto sheets of smooth leather called parchment. The sheets of parchment were piled together in a codex just like the papyrus codex. Wealthy people paid for beautiful copies to be made of the precious Scriptures. We can trust the Bible because faithful Christians kept on making careful copies of the Bible books through many centuries after Jesus went back to heaven.

## Teaching Tips

• Explore these Bible topics with your child: Paul the apostle quotes Luke as Scripture—1 Timothy 5:18, Luke 10:7; Peter says the letters of Paul are Scripture—2 Peter 3:15, 16; Paul calls his own writing "the word of God"—1 Thessalonians 2:13.

• Have you started learning the books of the Bible with your child? Besides learning them as a song (see teaching tips on page 8), you can start with the first five books, and after a few days, add five more. Keep adding more books until the list is complete.

• Do you already read short Bible passages to your child twice daily? Do you talk about them and see what can be applied to daily life? Consider starting now.

# Preserving the Bible

For hundreds of years, the Hebrew Bible was preserved very carefully. Copies were made by scribes called the *Masoretes*. *Masoretes* means traditions or habits. The Masoretes had a habit of following strict rules for copying the Hebrew Bible books, just like the scribes of earlier times. They were very careful not to make mistakes.

The Masoretes did make a few changes to the Hebrew Bible, however. In a few places where an Old Testament prophet predicted the coming of Jesus, the scribe changed the wording. Some Jewish people did not accept Jesus when He came to earth. They also did not want to accept the prophecies about Jesus in the Old Testament. To the Masoretes, it seemed acceptable to change God's Word to fit their belief. Of course, Jesus really did come to earth. He lived and died to save us from our sins. Changing the words of the Hebrew Bible cannot make Jesus go away!

Today, many examples of the Bible codex still exist. The most famous of the early copies of the Bible are the Codex Vaticanus and the Codex Sinaiticus. Codex Vaticanus was written about the year A.D. 350 on a type of thin, smooth leather called *vellum.*

The Codex Sinaiticus was written at roughly the same time. The story of how the codex was found is very exciting. Constantin von Tischendorf, a German explorer, visited the monastery of St. Catherine at Mount Sinai (see picture) in 1844. Tischendorf found sheets of vellum in a box of scraps. On the vellum pages were parts of the books of 1 Chronicles, Jeremiah, Nehemiah, and Esther. The monks were using the sheets as kindling to start fires in their fireplace! Tischendorf took the vellum sheets back to Germany. He visited the monastery again in 1859 and found an almost complete codex of the Bible, now called the Codex Sinaiticus.

# Jerome the Scribe

Once upon a time, I lived in a house with three roommates. My roommates' names were Jaime, Nestor, and Daniel. They know how to speak Spanish and English. I know how to speak English but not Spanish. Sometimes those three guys spoke Spanish to each other, and I did not have a clue what they were saying. When my roommates were talking about me in Spanish, I wished I knew that language!

Jesus knew the Aramaic language when He lived on this earth. His disciples and the Israelites spoke Aramaic, too, but educated people at that time spoke Greek. To make things more complicated, the Romans who ruled Israel during Jesus' time spoke a language called Latin.

Having to deal with three different languages would be confusing, wouldn't it?

We can trust the Bible because God caused the sacred books to be translated into the right language at the right time. After Jesus went back to heaven, more and more people in the world spoke Latin as their main language. The New Testament books were written in Greek. The Old Testament books were available in Greek and Hebrew. But the people who spoke Latin wanted to read the Bible too. Those early Christians needed a Latin translation of the Bible.

By the year A.D. 200, several people had translated some of the Greek Bible books into Latin. Those people lived in different places far apart, and some of them did not do a very good job of translating the books. The early Christian church leaders decided that Christians needed a good Latin Bible without mistakes in it. A godly, well-educated man named Jerome got the job of making that Latin translation.

As a young man, Jerome became a Christian because of a dream. In the dream, a voice asked him what he believed in. He replied, "I am a

Christian." But the voice said to him, "You are telling a lie. You are a Ciceronian." Now, what did that mean? Deep in his heart, Jerome preferred the beliefs of pagan writers like Cicero. When he woke up from the dream, Jerome realized his need for Jesus.

About the year A.D. 382, Jerome moved to the city of Rome. He worked as a scribe and translator for a church leader named Damasus. In this job, Jerome translated the four Gospels from Greek to Latin. He may have finished translating all of the New Testament in Rome. No one knows for sure.

Sadly, Damasus died in A.D. 384, and Jerome had no job in Rome anymore. He moved to the town of Bethlehem in Palestine. In the very town where Jesus was born, Jerome continued his work of translating the Bible into Latin. He finished the work on the Old Testament there.

For the rest of his life, Jerome wrote about the Bible and shared it with others. His Bible translation gradually became the accepted Latin Bible for all Christians. Jerome's Latin translation was the main Christian Bible for more than a thousand years. Today, we still have about ten thousand copies that are stored in different places around the world.

**This Bible is illuminated with a picture of Jerome, translating the Bible from Greek into Latin.**

In the year 1546, Christian church leaders had a meeting called the *Council of Trent*. They gave Jerome's Bible the name *Vulgate*. *Vulgate* means common. By giving the Bible this name, the leaders were saying that this most common Bible was the official Bible of the church. We can trust the Bible because God appointed the scribe Jerome to make a careful translation into Latin for the hundreds of years when most Christians spoke the Latin language.

## Words from Jerome's translation

Many of the words we read in the English Bible today come from Jerome's Latin translation. You may recognize words such as *ministry, conversion, congregation,* and *Calvary.* These are words that Jerome used. Hundreds of years after Jerome died, English translators kept many of Jerome's words because they are better than other words they could have chosen. When you read the Bible, watch for words that end in *-tion.*

**This illumination comes from the Winchester Bible. In this painting, God is talking with the prophet Jeremiah.**

That is a clue the word came from Latin and is most likely a word from Jerome's Vulgate Bible.

Copies of Jerome's Latin Bible had to be written by hand. One scribe could only write one copy at a time. The scribes who made copies of the Latin Vulgate Bible believed that they had a sacred job given to them by God. Many of the copies contain beautiful pictures called *illuminations.*

# Teaching Tips

- Explore these Bible topics with your child: God's Word available to everyone—Mark 13:31; the Bible alive and strong—Hebrews 4:12.
- Create an illumination with your child. Find examples by doing a Google image search for such key words as "Bible illuminations." Choose a Bible passage that you will illuminate. Sketch out a shape for the words on a sheet of plain paper, leaving gaps for a large opening capital letter and/or spots for pictures and decorations. Write the Bible verses inside the shape you created. If your child can write, have him or her do it. Use markers, crayons, colored pencils, or paint for the illumination.
- Look at John 6:68 with your child. This verse helps a child to understand why Christians trust the Bible as the Word of God. The disciples who spent time with Jesus in person had come to believe that He was truly the Son of God. The words He said were true. The Bible contains the words of God and is therefore what we can and should believe as the absolute truth.

# The "Almost" Bible Writers

Fruit is one of the best gifts God created for us, right? Who doesn't love to bite into a juicy red plumcot? Or a tasty ugli fruit? Perhaps your favorite is a tangelo.

Hey, wait a minute. Those aren't real fruits, are they? Yes, they are *hybrid* fruits. That means a mix of two different kinds. A plumcot is part plum, part apricot. The ugli fruit, grown in Jamaica, is a mix of orange, grapefruit, and tangerine. What is a tangelo? It is a hybrid of a tangerine and a pomelo or grapefruit.

Does it surprise you that some books were not included in the Bible because they were not God's pure truth? Just like a mixed-up fruit, those books were a mix of truth and made-up ideas. We can trust the Bible because, when it came time to decide which books belonged in the Bible, God helped His people to keep some books out.

The *Apocrypha* is one group of books not chosen for the Bible. The books were written during the years after the last prophet of Israel, Malachi, until the time of Jesus. Several of the books are adventure stories.

The book of Tobit tells the story of a good man from Nineveh named Tobit, who became blind. His son Tobias traveled to the land of Media and found a cure for his father's blindness. Along the way, Tobias met a woman named Sarah and married her. He came home and helped cure his father, and everyone lived happily ever after. The book is not a message from God.

The apocryphal book of Sirach has wisdom sayings like the book of Proverbs. Then there are the history books of the Maccabees. Those two books tell about the Hasmonean family. They ruled the Israelites until the Romans took over Jerusalem in the year 63 B.C.*

---

* B.C. stands for Before Christ, and it means the number of years before the time of Jesus Christ. Christ's time was about two thousand years ago, so the date 63 B.C. means two thousand sixty-three years ago.

One long book, with four sections, is full of stories about Baruch, who was the faithful scribe of the prophet Jeremiah. Another book called Bel and the Dragon tells about the prophet Daniel killing a big snake.

Under the guidance of God's Holy Spirit, the early Christians knew which books were inspired messages from God. They knew that the Apocrypha books were not inspired.

Another kind of book that didn't get to be in the Bible is pseudepigrapha. No, they are not books about pigs. The books have names like Moses, Solomon, and Enoch. But they were not written by those men. The writers of the pseudepigrapha were not prophets called by God. They did not have inspiration from God's Holy Spirit.

Pretend gospel books were written after the time of Jesus. They go against the teachings of Jesus and are not good to read. Books like the Gospel of Thomas and the Gospel of Judas sound like inspired books. But the words in them are not God's truth. None of the Bibles today have these books in them.

We can trust the Bible because God guided His people to know which books are Scripture and which ones are not. We can trust the Bible because it was not one man or one small group of people who decided which books should be in the Bible. Over many years and at several meetings, large numbers of Christians agreed on which books were inspired by God. And together, God's people understood which books were the "almost" Scriptures. They figured out the books that did not belong in the Bible.

# Teaching Tips

• Explore these Bible topics with your child: Jesus said the Holy Spirit will tell us what is true—John 16:13; Paul recommends the plain truth about God—2 Corinthians 4:2; David promised God he would stand up for truth—Psalm 101.

• Today, the Bible used by the Roman Catholic Church has the Apocrypha books in it. Why does one Bible have the Apocrypha and another Bible does not? Catholic church leaders decided to keep the Apocrypha, but the church does not count them as inspired Scripture.

# The Bible in the Middle Ages

Have you heard of the Middle Ages in history? We call the years from about A.D. 500* to 1500 the Middle Ages. They were one thousand years long. You may wonder, Why are they called the Middle Ages? What are they in the middle of? Two important things happened that help us understand why those years are called the middle.

The Romans ruled the Jewish people at the time of Jesus. The Jews hated the Romans. They wanted to have a Jewish king instead of the Roman emperor. After Jesus went back to heaven, the Roman emperors persecuted the early Christians and tried to destroy their copies of the Scriptures. The Roman Empire was powerful and cruel.

---

* A.D. stands for *Anno Domini*, which is Latin for "year of our Lord," and it means the number of years since the time of Jesus Christ. That was two thousand years ago, so the date A.D. 500 means one thousand five hundred years ago.

Then, in the year A.D. 476, the Roman emperor, Romulus Augustus, was replaced by a chief of what are called *barbarian tribes*. That was the end of the Roman Empire. From then on, a different set of people ruled the countries where the Bible

A replica of the Gutenberg press in Carson, California

was put together. The Middle Ages began when the Romans were no longer in charge.

A thousand years later, more big changes came. In a short period of time, most of the countries in Europe and the Middle East were conquered by new rulers. Most important of all, Johannes Gutenberg invented a printing press that used moveable type. A printing press meant many more people could get knowledge from books. The spread of knowledge ended the Middle Ages.

We can trust the Bible because the Bible did not stop with the Greek and Latin copies that the early Christians read. God made sure His Word was translated into languages and carried to many parts of the world even before printing presses.

The barbarian tribes that conquered the Romans were called *Goths*. The Goths were warriors. They spent a lot of time raiding cities and towns and conquering them. Don't they sound like a group of people that needed the Bible? I think so. God provided a way for the Bible to reach them.

The Goths raided a town in what is now the country of Turkey. They captured a young Christian woman and took her away with them. The woman married a Goth warrior and had a son. She named her son Ulfilas, which means "little wolf." Ulfilas did not become a warrior like his father. He got a good education and became a Christian minister.

Ulfilas began his Christian ministry to the Goths when he was thirty years old. He had a big difficulty to overcome: the Goths did not have an alphabet and did not read or write anything at all. Ulfilas created a Gothic alphabet from some Greek and Latin letters. He spent many years translating the Septuagint and the Greek New Testament into the Gothic language. The Gothic Bible written by Ulfilas was read by thousands of people all over Europe.

Here is another reason we can trust the Bible. In times of peace and war, God guided ministers to prepare the Bible for every group of people. No matter how dangerous the world became,

**A Verse to Remember:**
*"When you heard his message from us, you accepted it as the word of God, not the words of humans"* (1 Thessalonians 2:13, NCV).

the Bible was always there to help people know Jesus and find salvation.

So the Bible we have is the fruit or the results of what scribes and ministers did in the Middle Ages. We cannot know who the people were unless we look into history and find out. We can trust the Bible when we learn how many people obeyed God's call to translate and copy the sacred books.

About the same time Ulfilas was working on a Bible for the Goths, a *monk* named Mesrop created an alphabet for the language of Armenia. (A monk is a man who dedicates his life to the things of God. He chooses not to have a family or a house of his own.)

The monk Mesrop wanted to give the Bible to the Armenian people in their own language. With the help of some other monks, Mesrop finished the Armenian Bible in about five years. He also invented an alphabet for the Georgian language and one for the Albanian language. Other monks were able to translate the Bible into those two languages because of Mesrop's help.

Two brothers, Cyril and Methodius, were highly educated Christian missionaries from Thessalonica, Greece. They went to live in the country then known as Moravia. The people in

The beautiful pictures that scribes and monks painted or drew on the pages of the Bible are called *miniatures*. That does not mean they are small pictures. The Latin word *miniare* means to color with red. The Greek and Roman scribes who wrote the earliest Bibles created pictures only in red and black. Later, they used many types of paint, including gold.

Moravia, known as Slavs, had copies of the Bible in Greek and Latin. But they did not know those languages. Slav people also had no alphabet or writing in their own language.

Cyril created a Slavic alphabet. The brothers began to translate the Greek Bible into Slavic. Cyril became ill and died, but Methodius carried on and completed the Slavic Bible. Some years later, the Slavic Christians moved away from Moravia. They took their copies of the Bible to countries like Bulgaria, Romania, and Russia. The alphabets of many eastern European countries are called Cyrillic. Those alphabets are named after the faithful monk Cyril.

A monk named Alcuin was born in York, England, in A.D. 735. Alcuin was a good student and writer. In A.D. 796, King Charlemagne of France made Alcuin the *abbot,* or chief monk, of the Tours monastery where many monks spent all of their days writing new copies of the Bible.

The monks had always written in big capital letters, called *majuscules.* That kind of writing took a long, long time. Alcuin invented smaller letters that connected to each other. The letters were called *minuscules.* Now the monks could copy a Bible correctly twice as fast as when they wrote in majuscules.

In many areas of Europe, the people had parts of the Bible translated into their spoken language. But most of them did not have a good and complete Bible. In the 1100s, groups of Christians in the Netherlands, Germany, and France urged people to live according to everything the Bible says. The people could only do that if they had Bibles in their native languages.

Just like the old days when people wanted Latin instead of Greek Bibles, now people needed German and French Bibles.

By this time, the head of the Christian church was called the *pope.* In the year 1199, Pope Innocent decided that people should not have the Bible in their own languages. Only the leaders called *bishops* could own a Bible and read it to people. The pope wanted the church to control the reading of the Bible.

Some Christian groups like the Albigensians and the Waldensians continued to copy and give away parts of the Bible in their native languages. The church authorities did not like this at all.

## Teaching Tips

• Explore these Bible topics with your child: God's work always wins—Proverbs 19:21; Jesus called Paul to carry the gospel to kings and foreigners—Acts 9:15; Daniel was faithful while he worked for a foreign king—Daniel 6:5; Jonah obeyed God and spoke for Him—Jonah 3:4, 5; Jeremiah the faithful prophet—Jeremiah 38:1–13; Philip helped a man understand the gospel—Acts 8:26–39.

• Go to http://commons.wikimedia.org/ and search for illuminated Bibles. Guess what Bible story each picture shows. Try drawing your own illuminated Bible pictures.

# The Waldensians

A strange thing happened to the Christian church in the Middle Ages. The church and its leaders became very wealthy. The leaders owned fancy buildings and homes. They had expensive jewels and more money than they needed. After a thousand years, the church that Jesus started had changed. It had become greedy and selfish. Isn't that sad?

Around the year 1130, a brave monk named Arnold decided to speak up for Jesus. He asked the church leaders to give everything away. He asked them to give away the money and the buildings and all the other riches. The church leader, Pope Innocent, hated that idea. He refused to give away anything at all. He also banished Arnold. That means he sent Arnold away from his job as a monk.

Other good men followed Arnold's example. They wanted to be unselfish like Jesus. A rich man named Waldes lived in the town of Lyons, France. Waldes asked the priest of the town how he could live like Jesus. The priest answered with the words of Jesus: "Go and sell everything you have. Give the money to those who are poor. . . . Then come and follow me" (Matthew 19:21, NIrV). Waldes gave some money to his wife and daughters. Then he sold everything he owned. He gave the money to the poor. From that time, Waldes spent his time preaching about Jesus.

Waldes did not have a French Bible. He paid someone to translate parts of the Bible into French. He learned many Bible verses by heart. That way, he could preach from memory. Many people listened to Waldes's preaching and agreed with him.

The church leader, called the bishop, in Lyons did not like what Waldes was doing.

> **A Verse to Remember:**
> *"[Jesus said] You carefully study the Scriptures because you think that they give you eternal life. Those are the same Scriptures that tell about me!"* (John 5:39, ICB).

In 1179, he ordered Waldes to stop preaching. Waldes went to see the pope in Rome. He asked the pope for permission to preach from the Bible. The pope said, "You can only preach if the bishop asks you to preach." The bishop had already said Waldes could not preach. What should Waldes do now? He went right on preaching from the Bible! He was sure that he must obey God rather than any person.

The people who believed Waldes's preaching were called the Waldensians. They lived all over France and Italy. In 1184, a new pope named Lucius said that the Waldensians were no longer members of the church. They had been kicked out. Were the Waldensians sad about this? No, they were not. They knew that it was most important to be true to God and the Bible.

The church leaders wanted to arrest the Waldensians to stop them from preaching. Many of the Waldensians moved to northern Italy to escape. They lived in beautiful valleys near the mountains called the Alps. Some of them grew crops, and others kept sheep and goats. All of the Waldensians, including the children, learned passages of the Bible. They sent missionaries to the towns nearby. The people wanted to share the truth of the Bible.

The Waldensians had strong faith in God. Some soldiers came to arrest them for preaching. The Waldensians moved into caves in the snowy mountains. Even today, you can visit a cave church where they worshiped.

Life became very difficult for the Waldensians. Some of them were hurt or killed. Still, they studied the Bible every day. Even though soldiers were chasing them, they did not give up.

We can trust the Bible because it teaches

All the Waldensians, including children, memorized Bible texts.

us to do what is right. The Bible has inspired faithful people to follow Jesus no matter how difficult it gets. People who turn their backs on God and the Bible do evil things. The Bible helps us to know what is good and pure and true. When we follow what the Bible says and share it with others, we are like the Waldensians, faithful to God always.

### A peddler shares God's Word

Philippe, a Waldensian peddler, led his donkey up the garden path to the tall wooden door. He knocked and waited. He was sure that a wealthy lady lived in the fine-looking house. She would probably want to buy silk cloth from him. Perhaps she would buy some of his precious gems too.

The heavy door creaked and squeaked as it opened. A manservant poked his head around the door. "What do you want?" he asked in French.

"Kind sir," Philippe replied. "I have fine silk and pure pearls for the lady of the house. Please allow me to speak to her."

"Come in and stand by the door," the manservant instructed him.

Philippe tied the donkey's halter to a post

**Entrance to cave church in the Alps**

and lifted a wooden box from its back. He stepped in through the doorway and stood still. The manservant pushed the heavy door shut and disappeared down a hallway.

Philippe looked around the foyer of the house. He noticed a picture hanging on the wall. It was a picture of Jesus. The picture was plain and simple, just Jesus by Himself. There were no fancy crosses or pictures of Jesus' mother, Mary, in it.

*That picture tells me something important,* Philippe thought to himself. *The people in this house seem to believe what the Bible says. They know the true way to worship God.* Philippe always wanted to share Jesus with people. But he had to be very careful. In the Middle Ages, when he lived, a person could be arrested for speaking the truth from the Bible.

Soon, a young lady in a long silk dress came toward Philippe. "Good afternoon," she said. "I am Margarite. What are you selling?"

"Good day, Lady Margarite. My name is Philippe." The peddler opened the box and drew out several rolls of shiny cloth. "I have these beautiful silks from India. Look at the pretty patterns and colors."

Margarite took one of the cloth rolls from Philippe. It was a beautiful bright red fabric. She felt the soft material. A smile came across her face.

"Would my lady like to buy this silk?" Philippe asked.

"Yes, I will buy it," Margarite said. The two agreed on a price for the silk cloth.

"I have more to show you," the old man said. He reached into his box again. He was searching for something at the bottom. His fingers found a small pouch and opened it. He drew out sev-

Waldensian peddlers shared God's Word.

eral pearls about the size of small marbles. The pearls seemed to glow in the afternoon light. Margarite's eyes widened. She took one of the pearls from his hand.

"Where did you get these beautiful pearls?" she asked.

"I know a pearl merchant in the city of Milan. His pearls come from the Arabian Sea," Philippe told her.

"They are lovely," Margarite said. "Perhaps another day."

So Philippe took her coins for the cloth. Before Margarite could say Goodbye, he raised his hand and said, "Dear lady, please consider one last treasure. There is something I would like to share with you."

Philippe took a small knife from his bag. He opened his coat. With the knife, he cut a few stitches in the seam. A sheet of paper slipped out into his hand. It had been hidden inside his coat. Quietly, quickly the peddler handed the sheet of paper to Margarite.

The words on the paper were Bible verses! Unlike many people of her time, Margarite knew how to read. In those days, very few people had books. Almost no one had a Bible of their own. The church did not allow anyone but the priests to read the Bible. Margarite had never seen any Bible texts at all. "How much money for this piece of God's Word?" she asked.

"Please keep your coins," Philippe said. "The Word of God is free." He smiled at her.

Philippe put his wares into the box. "Read the verses to your family," Philippe said. "Take the words of Jesus to heart and follow them." And he walked out the door.

Later that day, Lady Margarite sat in the great room of her father's house. She thought about the peddler she had met. He had not told her where he was from. But she could guess. She had heard about the peddlers and missionaries known as the Waldensians. In spite of the danger of arrest, they traveled across Europe. They sold fine things and quietly gave portions of God's Word to people.

The faithful Waldensians believed that God's Word is true. They believed that everyone can receive the good news about Jesus. Faithful people like Philippe worked hard to share it with everyone they met.

## Teaching Tips

- Explore these Bible topics with your child: The cost of following Jesus—Matthew 8:18–20; how to follow Jesus every day—Luke 9:23, 24; the reward for being faithful—Revelation 21:1–5.
- Two wonderful children's books tell the story of French Protestants who were faithful like the Waldenses: *No Peace for a Soldier* and *Any Sacrifice but Conscience*.

# The First English Bibles

When I was in school, a young woman asked me if people spoke English in England. I was puzzled by her question. It seemed she did not know that the English language came to America from England. You are reading or hearing this story in the English language. Did you ever think about that?

The Bible written in English has a long history. The followers of God in England knew that English people would best learn God's ways in their own language. We can trust the Bible because God helped and protected brave people who brought the Scriptures to those who speak English.

An English monk named Caedmon lived in the late 600s. Caedmon was afraid of singing up front in the monastery.

Do you like singing in front of a crowd? Caedmon did not like it. One evening he went to bed early to avoid being called on to sing. As he slept that night, Caedmon had a dream. An angel commanded him to make songs and poems about how the world was created. From then on, Caedmon wrote many poems, songs, stories, and sermons in English. All of his works were based on the great stories of the Bible. For many English people in Caedmon's time, that was the only Bible they had.

Caedmon wrote in what is called Old English. Today, we would find Old English hard to understand. It is much different than today's English. During the Middle Ages, several men translated parts of the Bible into Old English. Among those men of God were the Venerable Bede, Egbert, and King Alfred the Great.

About A.D. 1000, a bishop named Aelfric translated the first seven books of the Old Testament into Old English. At roughly the same time, someone whose name we do not know

**John Wycliffe**

translated the four Gospels into Old English. They are called the *Wessex Gospels.*

Starting about the year 1320, a man named Richard Rolle made a translation of the whole Bible. Richard Rolle was known as the Hermit of Hampole. Rolle spent many years quietly working on a northern English version of the Bible. Remember the Latin Bible called the Vulgate? That is the Bible he used for translation. Today, we would call Richard Rolle's language Middle English. Some of the words would seem strange to us, while other words are quite similar to today's English.

During the Middle Ages, the Roman Catholic Church had power over the people in England. The leaders of the church made the rules. Anyone who did not follow the rules could be arrested and perhaps executed. The leaders had come up with some rules that God does not like. They said, for instance, that church tradition was equal to the words of the Bible. They also said that no church member was allowed to have a Bible in their own language.

A very smart church leader in England named John Wycliffe became popular with the people. Why? Wycliffe began to disagree with the church's bad rules. He said, "Every Christian ought to study this book [the Bible] because it is the whole truth." For that, the people needed the Bible in English. Wycliffe and two of his friends, John Purvey and Nicholas of Hereford, took the Latin Vulgate Bible and created a translation. They wrote in simple, easy to understand English.

The church leaders were angry about Wycliffe's English Bible. But they did not stop him. Wycliffe was popular with thousands of English people. The

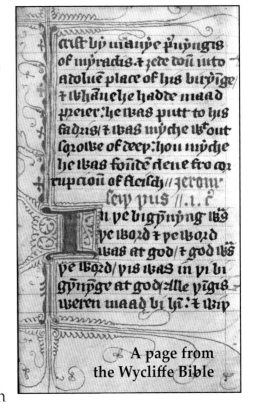

A page from the Wycliffe Bible

leaders did not dare to arrest or punish him.

John Wycliffe and his helpers finished the English New Testament in 1382. While working

People known as the Lollards were John Wycliffe's followers. Like the Waldensians in Europe, the Lollards were preachers who traveled often and preached from the Bible. They visited towns all over England. They gave away handwritten copies of parts of the Scriptures in English. This was against the orders of the Roman Catholic Church in England.

The name *Lollard* means "mutterer." The name was an insult. It was supposed to make the preachers look foolish. Instead,

the ordinary people of England welcomed the Lollards. They loved to hear the pure Bible message preached by Wycliffe's followers.

This cleft (*above*) or space between mountains is believed to be a place where Lollards worshiped in hiding.

on the Old Testament, Wycliffe became sick and died. Nicholas of Hereford finished the Old Testament in 1388.

Thirty years later, English church leaders did a very silly thing. They dug up Wycliffe's body and burned it. "That will be punishment for breaking our rules," they said. But it was far too late. Wycliffe was already dead. And the English Bible was spreading all around the country.

## Teaching Tips

- Explore these Bible topics with your child: Isaiah prophesies about bad church rulers—Isaiah 29:13–16; Jesus' warning about church leaders who turn bad—John 15:26–16:4; God wants His people to stand up for their faith—Jude 3.

- Look in a hymnal or other religious music books. See if you and your child can discover hymns based on the book of Psalms. (The Scriptural Allusions Index in the *Seventh-day Adventist Hymnal* can help you.) Read the words of the psalm and hymn aloud.

- Help your child write his or her own psalm, telling how great God is, what He is like, and why you love Him. The psalm doesn't have to rhyme or have any particular meter. However, psalms that do have meter or rhyme can be set to music or sung to a familiar tune.

- If you have some rubber stamps, show your child how to "print" with them. Show him or her how to care for the stamps and stamp pads. Look at the back of a word stamp. How is it like the metal type pictured on page 56?

# Gutenberg, Printing, and Bookmaking

Johannes Gutenberg made a great invention that changed the world. Gutenberg made cut-out shapes of all the letters of the alphabet, using pieces of metal. He could then put all the letter shapes in any order of words that he wanted. After he put ink on the letter shapes, he could press them on a piece of paper. Then all the words would appear on the paper, just like a potato print. Gutenberg's

Forty-eight Gutenberg Bibles still exist today. Only twenty-one of them have all their pages. Eleven Gutenberg Bibles are in museums and libraries in the United States. Two places you can see a real Gutenberg Bible are the Library of Congress in Washington, D.C., and the Huntington Library in California. The New York Public Library owns the Bible below. Gutenberg printed the Bibles with black ink. The color and

illustrations were added by hand later. The black-and-white picture is of Gutenberg in his print shop.

Photo © Kevin Eng

**Moveable type, the type that Gutenberg invented, has to be set backwards in order to print correctly. Can you read the words in this picture? "The quick brown . . ." is how it starts. The whole sentence makes more sense to someone who understands printing, but it is still fun to try to read. You can also hold this page up to a mirror and read the words in the mirror.**

invention is called *moveable type.*

Gutenberg made a printing press that could use his moveable type. He began to print whole books in a very short time. From that time on, no one would need to write every word on every single page of a book. Gutenberg could print the pages and make the books very quickly in comparison to copying them by hand.

Do you know which book Gutenberg printed first? A Bible! His large Bible was actually two books, with more than one thousand two hundred pages altogether. The Bible version he used was the Latin Vulgate Bible, a Bible used a lot in the Middle Ages.

Gutenberg created little letters in metal to make the words for all the pages. The letters were meant to look like handwriting, because that is what people were used to reading. Gutenberg actually made different letters to look like different people's handwriting.

One day Gutenberg had a disagreement with a businessman. The man had loaned him the money to print the Bibles. A court decided that Gutenberg's printing press should be given to that man, Johann Fust. Sadly, Gutenberg had to start over in his printing business. However, he printed more Bibles later, on a smaller press. Gutenberg never lost his desire to print Bibles.

Do you remember those bad rules the church

> **A Verse to Remember:**
> *"Use the truth to make . . . [my disciples] holy. Your word is truth"*
> *(John 17:17, NIrV).*

leaders made? One rule said that no one could own a Bible except the priests and bishops of the church. But now, with the printing press, hundreds of Bibles could be printed in a short time. There was no way the church leaders could control all of those Bibles.

The Gutenberg Bibles were expensive, almost three years' wages in the Middle Ages. But in time the printing press allowed many people to own their own Bibles, when before almost no one had a Bible.

Johannes Gutenberg's invention of moveable type changed the whole world. We can trust the Bible because God made sure that the printing press brought Bibles to people everywhere who wanted to know about Him.

# Teaching Tips

- Explore these Bible topics with your child: The light of truth shines from God's people—Matthew 5:14, 16; the best use of printing and books—Matthew 28:18–20; what isn't the world big enough for?—John 21:25.
- Make potato prints. Help your child cut some raw potatoes in half. Press a miniature cookie cutter into the flat part of the cut potato. Use a sharp knife to cut away the potato around the shape, so that shape sticks up out of the potato. Or, draw some simple shapes on a piece of paper.

Cut out the shapes and put each of them on the flat part of the cut potato. Cut away the potato around the shape. Finally, you need some different colors of paint or ink. Pour each color onto a plate. Then dip the potato shape in the paint, plant it firmly on a blank piece of paper, and you will see the shape painted on the paper. Maybe add some glitter. You can make beautiful art this way!

- Make your own book. You will need paper strips about eighteen inches long and three to four inches wide. One side of the paper should be plain enough to write or draw on. Fold the paper strip in half width-wise. Unfold the strip and fold both ends in so they touch the center crease. Unfold the strip and lay it out so you can see all four sections. Choose a side to begin folding your accordion. These instructions will start on the right, but you may start on the left if you like. Fold the right edge of the strip so it lines up with the nearest crease. Leave the edge folded. Take the right crease and fold it so it lines up with the center crease. You should have an even zigzag pattern of folds on the right side. Repeat on the left side. Glue ribbon across one cover so the book can be tied closed. Now you get to write or draw in it!

# Mr. Erasmus, the Student of Greek

Do you remember what the Middle Ages were? They were the years between A.D. 500 and 1500. During those years, people who liked to read and study books started a new kind of school. They called it a *university*. The first universities were church schools. The students who studied books in the universities were called *scholars*.

You may remember also that the leader of the church was called the pope. A pope named Julius II was more interested in money than following Jesus. To get more money, Pope Julius sold *indulgences*. What was an indulgence? It was a piece of paper that said a person would get less punishment for committing a sin.

Can you believe that? People paid money for their sins, instead of just asking God to forgive them! Pope Julius tricked people into doing that.

Some scholars knew that selling indulgences went against the Bible. They began to think, *How can we help the problem? What can we do?* They wondered if the problem might be the Latin Bible the pope was using. Perhaps they could make some important corrections to the Latin Bible.

Do you remember what languages were used to write the original Bible books? They were Hebrew and Greek. Some scholars of the Middle Ages learned Hebrew and Greek. They found old scrolls and books of the Bible in Hebrew and Greek. They decided to make new translations of the Bible.

The first scholar who made some corrections to the Latin Bible was Lorenzo Valla. When he had a New Testament printed with the corrections in it, the church leaders of his city became very angry. They did not want anyone to see that they were doing bad things.

Mr. Erasmus *(far left)* made what today we call a *Parallel Bible*. Get a magnifier to see if you can figure out which column is Greek and which is Latin in Erasmus's New Testament. (The page on the left is from the book of Revelation).

About fifty years later, another scholar decided to try fixing the Latin Bible. His name was Desiderius Erasmus. Let's call him Mr. Erasmus.

Mr. Erasmus was a monk who did not like living in a monastery. He studied the Greek language and became a scholar instead. Mr. Erasmus printed a new kind of New Testament. On one side of the page was the original Greek language. On the other side was a corrected version of the Latin New Testament. This New Testament could not be used by the church leaders to do tricks like selling indulgences.

Mr. Erasmus did not want to make trouble. Instead, he wanted the pope and other church leaders to do what is right. We can trust the Bible because God inspired Mr. Erasmus and the scholars of the Middle Ages to make sure the Latin Bible was correctly translated. The scholars

helped put a stop to the bad things church leaders were doing. The scholars made new and better translations of the Bible.

### Why our Bibles have chapters and verses

Stephen Langton, a teacher in Paris, was one of the first people to divide the books of the Bible into chapters. He did this in the year 1227. Later, Mr. Langton became the archbishop of Canterbury in England.

In the 1500s, a scholar and printer named Robert Estienne lived in Paris. The Latin version of his name was Robert Stephanus. He printed Bibles with helpful notes. The notes helped the reader understand what the Bible verses meant. Robert put his Latin name, Stephanus, on the Bibles he printed.

Some church leaders in Paris wanted to stop Mr. Estienne from printing his Bible. He moved to the city of Geneva in Switzerland. There he was free to print Bibles with helpful notes.

In the year 1551, Mr. Estienne started to do something different. He put chapters and verses into all of the New Testament books he printed. In 1555, he put chapters and verses into the Old Testament books. We still have those same chapters and verses in our Bibles today.

## Teaching Tips

• Explore these Bible topics with your child: A Bible verse that says in old Latin, "do penance"—Mark 1:15; the good way that Scripture helps—2 Timothy 3:16, 17; an instruction to follow Jesus, not tradition—Colossians 2:8.

• Continue (or begin) learning the books of the Bible in order so that your child may become familiar with using the Bible and is able to find verses quickly. An audio file of "The Books of the Bible" song by Alfred P. Gibbs is available at www.wholesomewords.org.

# Tyndale and the First English Bibles

Have you ever gotten in trouble when you did nothing wrong? Did you feel angry and upset because someone said you were mean or broke a toy or something like that? And you really didn't do it! When that happens, you want things to be put right.

William Tyndale was an Englishman who got into trouble for doing what was right. Tyndale believed that the Bible is the true Word of God. He also believed that the Bible tells the truth about salvation. He believed that he should obey God and the Bible no matter how much other people hated him for it.

As a young man, Tyndale studied at two universities in England named Oxford and Cambridge. After he finished his studies, he became a priest in a church, which is something like a pastor. Do you know what William Tyndale was best at learning? He learned languages easily. Tyndale became an expert in seven different languages, including Greek and Hebrew. He was the best person in his time to create a whole translation of the Bible in English.

Tyndale asked the bishop of London, Bishop Tunstall, to let him translate the Bible into English. The bishop said, Absolutely not! (Remember that bad church leaders did not want regular people to understand the Bible because the church leaders were not following what the Bible said to do.)

Tyndale believed the Bible in English was needed. So, in the year 1524, he moved from England to Germany. There he could safely translate the Greek New Testament into English.

When the New Testament was finished,

> **A Verse to Remember:**
> *"Blessed are you when people make fun of you and hurt you because of me" (Matthew 5:11, NIrV).*

the books himself and had them burned.

You might think that was a sad end to the New Testament books in English. But God was watching over them. Bishop Tunstall did not know that he was buying the books from a friend of William Tyndale. Most of the money paid by Bishop Tunstall went right back to Tyndale! With that money, Tyndale printed many more of the New Testament books.

A short time later, Tyndale moved to the city of Antwerp

**Tyndale's** *(above left)* **last words were said to have been this prayer, "Lord! Open the King of England's eyes." That king** *(right)* **was Henry the Eighth. God answered Tyndale's prayer in a mighty way. Soon English Bibles were for sale all over England.**

Tyndale went to get books printed in the city of Cologne, Germany. But some evil men tried to stop the printing. Tyndale heard that the men were coming to the print shop to steal the books. He managed to take the half-printed books and escape from Cologne.

Tyndale finished printing the New Testament books in the German city of Worms. Then his friends smuggled thousands of the books into England. When Bishop Tunstall found out about the books, he was angry. He bought almost all of

in Belgium. He worked hard to translate the Old Testament from Hebrew into English. An Englishman named Henry Phillips came to visit Tyndale. Phillips said he liked the English translation of the Bible. The two men went for a walk in the town. While they were walking, two soldiers kidnapped Tyndale and put him in prison. Henry Phillips was really a spy who had been telling lies.

After more than a year in jail, Tyndale was executed as a heretic. That means he was killed for translating the Bible into English!

There was something Tyndale did not know when he died. The king of England, Henry VIII, was starting to change his mind. The king came to believe that people in England should have the Bible in English after all. Very soon after Tyndale's death, Bibles that used his English translation were available all over England.

William Tyndale was a very brave man. He believed that having a Bible in English was important. He also believed what the Bible says. We can trust the Bible written in English because Tyndale obeyed God even though it cost him his life.

### Martin Luther's German Bible

Martin Luther was a clever monk who lived in Germany at the end of the Middle Ages. Luther saw bad things happening in the church and spoke up for truth. The church rules said that a person could pay money for forgiveness from sin. But Luther knew from the Bible that church rules did not save anyone from sin. By studying the Bible carefully, Luther found out that if a person trusts Jesus to save them, then that person is saved from sin.

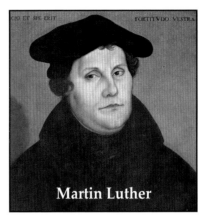

**Martin Luther**

Luther became famous for standing up to the bad rules of the Catholic Church. But he also translated the Bible from Greek and Hebrew to German. He finished the German version of the New Testament in eleven weeks. That is less than three months. The German words Luther used are so easy to understand that some German Bibles still use his wording today.

Luther's New Testament was very popular with the German people. It sold more than one hundred thousand copies in his lifetime.

The Old Testament took Luther twelve years to finish. He printed the complete German Bible in the year 1534.

**Teaching Tips**

• Explore these Bible topics with your child: Jesus talks about His suffering and death—Luke 9:22; God sends the Bible to people and always gets results—Isaiah 55:10, 11; faithful people will receive a great reward—Romans 8:18, 19.

# The King James Version of the Bible

You know how grown-ups sometimes use a word and you don't know what it means? When I was a young boy, I heard people say, "King James Version," when they talked about the Bible. I did not know what that meant, and nobody told me until I was older. It turns out that "King James Version" is the name of a famous and important Bible. We can trust the Bible because God inspired King James I to provide England with the most famous version of the Bible ever produced.

King James I

In 1567, James became king of Scotland. He was only a one-year-old baby. Of course, he did not wear a crown or rule the country then. That would have been silly. Important counts and dukes ruled Scotland for him until he was fifteen.

King James was friends with Elizabeth, the queen of England. Queen Elizabeth had no children. When she died of old age in 1603, King James of Scotland inherited her throne and became king of England as well.

King James knew that different groups of Christians in his kingdom were upset with each other. He wanted to bring them together. He called a meeting of all the religious leaders and scholars in England at his Hampton Court palace. What needs to change, King James asked, so that all of you will live together in peace? One answer, from a man named John Reynolds, was that the country needed a good English Bible that everyone would like to read. King James liked that idea very much.

Six months later, King James had organized

forty-seven of the best scholars in England. He split them up into six groups. The king gave them only a few requirements for their work on the new Bible: they must follow the old Bibles in Greek and Hebrew very carefully; they should use the English Bibles from past times to help them; and they were not to write lots of footnotes with their own opinions. King James wanted an accurate Bible that all Christian churches would like to use.

The translations took four years to complete. It took another three years to review the work and get the book ready to print. That may be almost as long as you have lived! But King James did not hurry the scholars. He wanted them to do the very best job they could on the sacred Scriptures.

How careful were those scholars? Very careful indeed. All of the people in each group would translate the same chapter. Then they showed their version to the others in their group. They all had to agree on the wording of the chapter. After the group finished a whole book of the Bible, it was given to twelve other people to review. That is a very careful method! No wonder it took so long to finish.

King James was a scholar himself. He wrote three good books of his own. He believed that the Bible is God's Word to people. In a letter to his oldest son, Prince Henry, King James wrote, "Diligently read His Word, and pray for the right understanding thereof."

The new Bible was finally complete in the year 1611. When it was printed, the Bible was dedicated to "the most high and mighty prince James." Although it was not printed with any name except the words *The Holy Bible*, it soon became known as the King James Version. So

**The King James Version of the Bible** *(above)* **was first printed in 1611, but twenty-four thousand changes to that first edition were made for the 1769 edition. The King James Bible today is basically the 1769 edition.**

now you know where that name came from.

*The Geneva Bible*

The Christians of England already had a Bible they liked very much—the Geneva Bible—when King James caused a new Bible to be translated. Why did that happen?

Queen Mary ruled England about fifty years before King James. She was a devoted Roman Catholic. During her reign, she made it illegal to have a Bible in English. Queen Mary persecuted those who disagreed with her. They were called *Protestants,* because they protested.

Some English Protestants moved to cities in Europe. In the city of Geneva, safe from Queen Mary, a man named William Whittingham printed a new translation of the Bible in English. It became known as the Geneva Bible.

After Queen Mary died, and her half-sister Elizabeth became queen, Bibles were allowed in England again. Then the Geneva Bible became a very popular book in England.

The Geneva Bible contained footnotes that King James did not like. The footnotes said that kings who did wrong would be punished by God. So when the religious leaders of England asked for a new Bible, King James realized that he could get rid of those footnotes.

The Geneva Bible continued to be popular for about forty years after the King James Bible was first printed. The King James Version was the most popular English Bible for three hundred twenty years after that.

# Teaching Tips

- Explore these Bible topics with your child: A famous piece of Bible poetry— Psalm 23; a famous phrase still used today—Matthew 5:41; an example of KJV English that's hard to understand—Psalm 119:147.
- Compare Psalm 23 or another favorite text in several Bible versions. If you don't have multiple verisons, go to www.BibleGateway.com where you can compare as many as five versions at a time. Be sure to include reading from the New International Readers' Edition (NIrV), preparared especially for early readers.

# The Bible Comes to America

Several times we've heard about God's people who moved from England to Europe. They moved away from home because they were being mistreated. Why were they mistreated? Because they loved and respected the Bible. It's hard to imagine that evil people would try to stop anyone from reading the Bible. Sadly, it has happened many times in history.

Puritans were Christians in England who wanted to follow the pure truth of the Bible. The Puritans had been mistreated in England. They refused to join the big Church of England. Too much of the religion of the Church of England did not follow the Bible. The Puritans needed to move away to somewhere safe, so they sailed to America in the year 1620. They sailed across the Atlantic Ocean in a ship called the *Mayflower*. The Puritans brought their Bibles with them. Which kind of Bible did they have? The Geneva Bible, which was popular in England in those days. Later, the King James Bible became the most used Bible in America.

English laws did not allow the Bibles to be printed in America. During the first hundred

The ship *Mayflower* took Puritans from England to the New World in 1620. On most voyages, the Mayflower was used for cargo, not passengers. On its most famous trip (the one carrying the Puritans), it carried one hundred two passengers plus a crew of twenty-five to thirty. The ship is estimated to have been the length of a basketball court and the width of half a basketball court. Its voyage took sixty-six days.

years of the American colonies, no English-language Bibles were printed there. All of the Bibles had to be printed in England. Then they were brought to America by ship. However, the Puritans had plenty of Bibles in English.

A missionary named John Eliot came to America from England in 1631. He was the pastor of a church in Roxbury, in the new American colony of Massachusetts. Eliot wanted to tell the Native Americans about Jesus. He learned the language of the Massachusetts Bay Native Americans. With the help of his church members, Pastor John Eliot began to preach to the Native Americans.

Not content with just preaching to the native people, Eliot wanted to give them a Bible. So he invented an alphabet for the language of the Native Americans. Then he began to trans-late the English Bible into Massachusett, the Native Americans' language. About the year 1663, John Eliot finished the whole Bible in Massachusett. So the first Bible produced in America was not an English Bible.

John Eliot not only provided a Bible for the Massachusetts Bay Native Americans. He also set up towns where the Native Americans could live as followers of Jesus. These were called "praying towns." The native people were given houses. They had gardens and cows. They learned crafts and studied the Bible. When they were ready, they were baptized as Christians. By the 1670s, about four thousand Native Americans lived in the praying towns. The Bible in their own language helped them to know Jesus and be faithful to Him.

About a hundred years later, the war of the American Revolution came. The people of the American colonies broke away from England and set up the United States of America. People who owned printing presses in America began to print their own English-language Bibles. They decided the laws of England did not apply to them anymore. In the new nation of the United States, different translations of the Bible could be freely printed anywhere. No evil people tried

**A Verse to Remember:**
*"The Good News about God's kingdom will be preached in all the world, to every nation. Then the end will come"* (Matthew 24:14, ICB).

**This stamp from Bulgaria celebrates Columbus's voyage and shows Columbus bringing Christianity to the New World.**

to stop the printers from printing their Bibles.

We can trust the Bible. God brought religious freedom to the United States so that anyone could own or print a Bible. And the words of the Bibles in America are the same as the Bibles of ancient times. God has kept His words safe and sound through the centuries of history.

*Christianity comes to North America*

The first people to bring Christianity to America were not English. Christopher Columbus came on his second voyage from Spain to explore America in 1493. He brought a Benedictine monk and some priests to evangelize the native people, whom he called Indians. We don't know if the priests had Bibles, but we know that they brought *catechisms* with them. A catechism

is a book that explains the beliefs of a church in a question-and-answer form.

In the 1500s, a group of Spanish missionaries set up almost four hundred missions in Mexico. Eventually, they built thousands of churches too. The Catholic Church did not permit people to have their own Bibles. So the missionaries did not print any Bibles. Although the missionaries did not provide Bibles, they taught Bible verses to the native people.

In the 1600s, French and Spanish explorers brought missionaries to what are now Florida and Texas. Along the coastlines, and even up the Mississippi River, they set up missions for preaching from the Bible.

# Teaching Tips

• Explore these Bible topics with your child: We must obey God rather than people—Acts 5:29; only God's truth makes us free—John 8:32; God speaks to us through the prophets of the past—Hebrews 1:1.

• Talk about what it means to be a missionary. Explain that God asks us all to share what we know about Him, and chooses men and women who have strong faith, have studied a lot about Him, and are willing to speak to strangers about Jesus to be full-time missionaries.

# Digging Up the Bible

When I was a boy, I lived in Africa. My family lived in a house on an acre of land. When we first moved there, the backyard was just dirt. One day, I was digging a deep hole in the dirt, and my shovel hit something hard. Soon I had dug out what looked like the bottom of a Roman column. I began to think, *How did that Roman column get under the dirt in my backyard in Africa?* I had no idea how it got there.

Photo © Steven G. Johnson

**The Black Obelisk shows King Jehu bowing to Assyrian King Shalmaneser, proving that the Bible story about King Jehu is true.**

There are some clever scientists who dig up old objects from the ground. They can sometimes tell how old the objects are. They might know who owned them or what they were used for. Those scientists are called *archaeologists.* They have dug up thousands of objects that tell us something about the Bible. They have found pieces of rock with lists of rules scratched on to them. They have dug up clay tablets with the names of kings pressed into them. They have found rings with the name of a Bible king on them. In a few places, archaeologists have unearthed the remains of an entire Bible town! We can trust the Bible because many objects found in the ground tell us something true about the Bible.

People called the Sumerians lived more than four thousand years ago. An archaeologist named Herbert Weld-Blundell dug up a four-sided column. On the cylinder was a list of Sumerian kings. What Bible story do you think is mentioned in that list? It is Noah's flood. According to the list, the kings before the Flood lived for many, many, many years. The kings after the Flood lived for a much shorter time. The list matches what the Bible says. You can see the Sumerian King List in the Ashmolean Museum in England.

A picture called the Beni Hasan tomb painting shows some Israelites on a journey. The picture was discovered on the wall of a tomb in Egypt. It is four thousand years old. From this picture, we know what people in the time of Abraham looked like and what clothes they wore. The people in the picture are carrying weapons. These are the same weapons (sword, bow and arrow, ax, spear) that Abraham and his people had. He and his 318 fighting men used these weapons to rescue Abraham's cousin Lot.

In 1846, an archaeologist named Austen Layard dug up a tall carved rock. It came to be

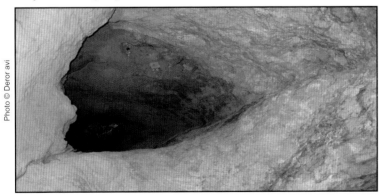

Photo © Deror avi

**Warren's Shaft is a tunnel under the city of Jerusalem. Archaeologists think that King David conquered Jerusalem by sneaking through this tunnel.**

known as the Black Obelisk. On the obelisk are some carved pictures and writing. One of the pictures shows a king bowing down to another king. The writing says that the king bowing down is King Jehu of Israel. King Jehu had made an agreement with King Shalmaneser III of Assyria. He had to pay money to Shalmaneser. Whether Jehu really bowed down to King Shalmaneser or not, no one knows. But the writing on the obelisk shows that the Bible verses in 2 Kings, which talk about King Jehu, are true.

In the year 1867, a British army officer named Charles Warren was sent to Jerusalem. The British government asked him to go. Warren's main job was to find out about the water supplies underneath the city. He found many tunnels and pools of water under the streets of Jerusalem.

With his helpers, Warren found a stone arch built by King Herod in the time of Jesus.

> **A Verse to Remember:**
> "LORD, you are our Father. We are the clay. You are the potter. Your hands made all of us" (Isaiah 64:8, NIrV).

Warren is most famous for finding what is called Warren's Shaft. It is a tunnel under the city that comes from the Gihon Spring. Archaeologists are pretty sure that King David used this shaft to sneak his soldiers into the city when he first conquered Jerusalem.

Charles Warren made another trip to Jerusalem with more helpers. He dug more than twenty-five holes in the ground. With them, he was able to show the ancient walls of the city, more than two thousand years old, from the time of King Herod.

We don't need carved rocks and broken pottery to prove that the Bible can be trusted. God proves Himself today by keeping His promises to you and me. However, the objects dug up from the ground help us to trust the Bible more. They give us something we can look at and say, "The Bible stories really happened. They are true!"

*How old is this pot?*

Do you remember the story of Job? After he lost his animals and his family, Job got sick with nasty boils on his skin. And then "he took for himself a potsherd with which to scrape himself" (Job 2:8, NKJV). Yuck! But I wondered, What is a potsherd?

It turns out that a potsherd is a piece of broken pottery. Archaeologists love potsherds. They collect hundreds of these pieces of broken pottery as they dig. From the pattern and shape of the pottery, the scientist can tell how old it is. That way they can know roughly the date of any other object they dig up in the same layer of dirt. It is because of potsherds that we know how old the Black Obelisk and other important objects are. Potsherds may seem like the trash of ancient people, but they are extremely helpful to us.

## Teaching Tips

• Explore these Bible topics with your child: Abraham uses his weapons—Genesis 14; David sneaks into Jerusalem—2 Samuel 5:8; the adventures of King Jehu—2 Kings 10.

# The Dead Sea Scrolls

Muhammad Ahmed al-Hamed, known by his nickname Muhammad the Wolf, climbed among the rocks and cliffs in the hot sun. The fifteen-year-old shepherd was searching for a lost goat. He and his cousin Jum'a saw some holes in the cliffs. Perhaps the goat fell into a cave, Jum'a suggested. He threw a few rocks into the holes.

Instead of hearing a bleating goat, the boys heard the crash of breaking pottery. After a few minutes of climbing, Muhammad the Wolf fell through a hole and landed in a cave! In the dim light, the boy saw a tall clay jar. Reaching in, he pulled out several scrolls. The scrolls were long pieces of leather on a roller, with Hebrew letters written all over them. What had he found?

In that year of 1946, the shepherd boys were living near the ancient village of Qumran. That is about seven miles from the Bible town of Jericho and one mile from the Dead Sea. The boys did not know that they had found scrolls

**This modern shepherd probably looks and dresses very much like the shepherd who discovered the Dead Sea Scrolls sixty-six years ago. His work herding animals is probably very much the same too.**

hidden by the Essenes, a group of religious people who lived in the time of Jesus. The two boys took the scrolls back to the camp where their Bedouin family was living. The family hung the scrolls on a tent pole until they could decide what to do with them.

The boys' family tried to sell the scrolls to a dealer in the town of Bethlehem. A dealer is someone who buys precious things and tries to sell them to collectors. But the dealer said No. He saw no value in the scrolls. At a nearby market, the family met a Christian man from Syria who agreed to buy the scrolls. After some bargaining, the family received twenty-nine dollars for the scrolls. The scrolls ended up in a monastery in Jerusalem. An American archaeologist, John Trever, was shown the scrolls in 1948. He took photographs and wrote a newspaper story.

> **A Verse to Remember:**
> *"God has made a great many promises. They are all 'Yes' because of what Christ has done"*
> *(2 Corinthians 1:20, NIrV).*

Soon the rest of the world began to hear about these scrolls.

What was on the scrolls? Parts of the Bible written in the Hebrew language. John Trever realized that the scrolls were written about the time of Jesus, or even before that. So they were very, very old copies of the Old Testament books.

Up until then, the oldest copies of Hebrew Bible books that anyone knew about were about one thousand years old. The shepherd boy, Muhammad the Wolf, had found scrolls of the Bible that were two thousand years old! Scholars, Christians, Jews, archaeologists, even kings and prime ministers were excited about this amazing find.

Which Bible books are written on the scrolls? Parts of every Old Testament book except the book of Esther can be found on the Dead Sea Scrolls. Some of them, like the book of Isaiah, are complete, while many of the scrolls have only part of a Bible book. In some cases, there are many copies of the same book. For instance, thirty-nine copies of the Psalms have been found.

Scholars have compared the Dead Sea Scrolls with the scrolls written out by the Masoretes, the Jewish scribes of later years. Even though the scrolls were written hundreds of years apart, in far distant places, they are almost exactly the same! Because of the Dead Sea Scrolls, we know that the words put into the Bible books are true. We can trust the Bible because God caused the books to be copied and recopied so very carefully.

### More about the scrolls

The Essenes were a group of Jewish people who decided to live apart from everyone else. The people built houses in a group and kept to themselves. They lived at Qumran from about 250 B.C. until

The cave entrance seen here is to cave number four where most of the Dead Sea Scrolls were found.

the Roman army destroyed their settlement around A.D. 68. The Dead Sea Scrolls are probably part of the Essenes' "library."

The Essenes hid their scrolls in the caves to preserve them in case of an attack. It is almost certain that when the Roman army came near to Qumran, the Essenes put their scrolls into the pottery jars and hid them, hoping to come back and find them later. Sadly, all of the Essene people were killed.

A famous scroll found in cave number three is called the Copper Scroll. The scroll is made of thin copper and was about eight feet long originally. The writing gives directions for finding gold, silver, and other treasure buried in the desert. But no one can understand the directions, which are unclear and incomplete. Many people have searched, but the treasure has not been found. You can see the Copper Scroll in Amman, Jordan.

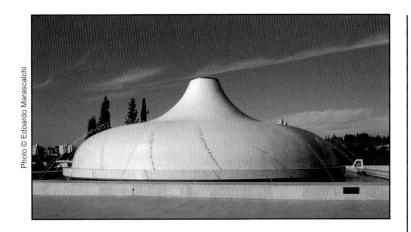
Photo © Edoardo Marascalchi

Shrine of the Book *(pictured, left)*, was built in Jerusalem.

The scrolls are very fragile so the museum only puts a few of them are put on display at any given time, but now, you can actually see the scrolls on the Internet!

# Teaching Tips

• Explore these Bible topics with your child: Look to God for faith, not to people—Romans 3:3, 4; God's promises can be trusted—2 Corinthians 1:18–20; King David's claim about God—Psalm 18:30.
• Go online to see the digital copies of the Dead Sea Scrolls, the oldest Bible manuscripts in existence. They are easily found by searching Google for "digital dead sea scrolls." You will find the scrolls as well as historical background information and short explanatory videos.

All of the Dead Sea Scrolls found in the first five years after their discovery were put on sale in New York in 1954. The man who secretly bought them for $250,000, Yigael Yadin, was the son of a professor in Jerusalem, Eleazar Sukenik, who had bought one of the first scrolls ever found. Yadin brought all of the scrolls to Israel. A special museum for the scrolls, called the

The Great Isaiah Scroll is the best preserved of the biblical scrolls found at Qumran. It contains the entire book of Isaiah in Hebrew,  apart from some small damaged parts. The scroll is very large: twenty-four feet long by eleven inches high.

# The Bibles of Today

Have you ever said to your mother, "Shall I compare thee to a summer's day"? If you have, she probably wondered why you said the word *thee*.

About four hundred years ago in the time of King James, people said thee instead you. Many English words back in those days were different than what we say today. That is why we have a difficult time reading some of the verses in the King James Bible.

Listen to this verse in the book of Mark: "Why reason ye, because ye have no bread? perceive ye not yet, neither understand? have ye your heart yet hardened?" (Mark 8:17). Try saying the last sentence very fast.

The King James Bible is a very inspiring and beautiful version of God's Word for us. But four hundred years after it was first printed, it is getting hard to read. You can imagine, then, that some people in the last hundred years wanted to make a Bible with modern English words. That is exactly what happened.

The King James Bible, as good as it is, has another problem. King James's scholars did a very good job with what they had, but their Bible was translated from Hebrew and Greek copies that were not very good.

Much later, some scholars in the 1800s found very old versions of the Hebrew Old Testament and the Greek New Testament. These old versions had much better Hebrew and Greek in them than the ones used for the King James Bible.

Here's the thing to remember: the older the Hebrew and Greek copies of the Bible, the better they are for making an English translation.

Scholars who translate Bibles today have some big help that the men and women in King James's time did not have. First of all, scholars today know the Hebrew and Greek languages

> **A Verse to Remember:**
> *"God's word is alive and working"* (Hebrews 4:12, ICB).

better than anyone did in King James's time. Also, they have the older copies of the Hebrew and Greek Bibles that are written better. We can trust the Bible because, through the centuries, God has helped scholars to make the Bible more accurate, not less.

Work on the first modern English Bible began in 1879. Scholars from England and the United States came up with the Revised Version. This Bible was based on the King James Version, but the words and sentences were much easier to understand. From the Revised Version, which was first printed in 1885, several later Bible versions came about.

A different group of people, known as the American Bible Society, got some scholars together. They made something called the Good News Bible, also known as Today's English Version. The purpose of it was to make reading the Bible very simple and enjoyable for everyone.

Because of the Dead Sea Scrolls and some other discoveries, some Christian leaders decided it was time for a brand-new translation of the English Bible. A large group of scholars from several countries began work in the 1960s on a Bible that became known as the New Inter-

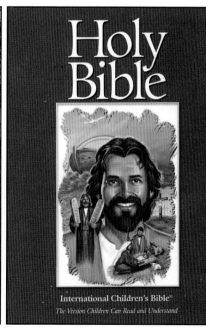
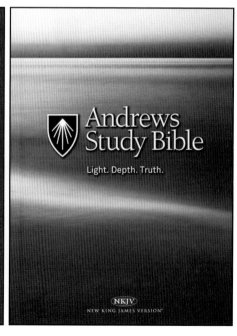

**Two children's Bibles you might have in your home: the NIrV and the ICB. The Andrews University NKJV is a wonderful study Bible for grown-ups.**

national Version. Have you heard of it? Perhaps you have a New International Version Bible of your own. The NIV, as it is called, was very popular as soon as it was first printed in 1978. By 1987, it sold more copies than the King James Bible and has done so ever since. (The NIrV— New International Readers' Version—is the NIV made even easier to read. The NIrV and the ICB—International Children's Bible—are wonderful Bibles for Primary kids to read.)

You may be getting tired just hearing all of the names of different Bibles. You might ask, Why are there so many? The reason is that, in recent times, so many good Hebrew and Greek copies have been found, we now have good Bible versions that are piled up like treasures.

Just like the Bible writers of ancient times, Bible scholars of today want to make the best Bible possible, with words that bring glory to God. We can trust the Bible today because God has protected it and delivered it to us. It comes with the same message of salvation through Jesus that was written by His faithful prophets and scribes thousands of years ago.

## Teaching Tips

• Explore these Bible topics with your child: God's Word is true forever—Psalm 119:89; the Scriptures never go away—Isaiah 40:8; what we must do with the Bible—1 Timothy 4:13.

• Radio, television, printed books and magazines, and personal mission work are just some of the ways the Seventh-day Adventist Church is spreading the gospel. Check out these Web sites: www.adventistmission.org; www.awr.org; www.hopetv.org; www.afmonline.org.

• There are about 6,800 languages in the world today. Only 457 languages have the entire Bible available. About 1,211 languages have the New Testament only. Around the world, about 340 million people have no part of the Bible in their language at all. Wycliffe Bible Translators has been making translations of the Bible into languages all over the world since 1942. On their Web site (www.wycliffe.org), you will find resources for kids to learn about the work of Bible translators. Another way to give people the Bible can be found at www .megavoice.com.

# Books of the Bible in Order

| *Old Testament* | Isaiah | Acts |
|---|---|---|
| Genesis | Jeremiah | Romans |
| Exodus | Lamentations | 1 Corinthians |
| Leviticus | Ezekiel | 2 Corinthians |
| Numbers | Daniel | Galatians |
| Deuteronomy | Hosea | Ephesians |
| Joshua | Joel | Philippians |
| Judges | Amos | Colossians |
| Ruth | Obadiah | 1 Thessalonians |
| 1 Samuel | Jonah | 2 Thessalonians |
| 2 Samuel | Micah | 1 Timothy |
| 1 Kings | Nahum | 2 Timothy |
| 2 Kings | Habakkuk | Titus |
| 1 Chronicles | Zephaniah | Philemon |
| 2 Chronicles | Haggai | Hebrews |
| Ezra | Zechariah | James |
| Nehemiah | Malachi | 1 Peter |
| Esther | | 2 Peter |
| Job | *New Testament* | 1 John |
| Psalms | Matthew | 2 John |
| Proverbs | Mark | 3 John |
| Ecclesiastes | Luke | Jude |
| Song of Solomon | John | Revelation |